A JOURNAL *of* OCCURRENCES *along the* REBEL COAST

A Chronology of Revolutionary War Naval Events in the Waters South and West of Cape Cod

1775-1781

Frederick V. Lawrence, Jr.

HERITAGE BOOKS
2008

HERITAGE BOOKS
AN IMPRINT OF HERITAGE BOOKS, INC.

Books, CDs, and more—Worldwide

For our listing of thousands of titles see our website
at
www.HeritageBooks.com

Published 2008 by
HERITAGE BOOKS, INC.
Publishing Division
100 Railroad Ave. #104
Westminster, Maryland 21157

Copyright © 2008 Frederick V. Lawrence, Jr.

All rights reserved. No part of this book may be reproduced or transmitted in any form or by any means, electronic or mechanical, including photocopying, recording or by any information storage and retrieval system without written permission from the author, except for the inclusion of brief quotations in a review.

International Standard Book Numbers
Paperbound: 978-0-7884-4595-8
Clothbound: 978-0-7884-7159-9

This book is dedicated to the people
of Cape Cod and the Islands.

Table of Contents

List of Illustrations vii

Foreword ix
   About the Chronology ix
   Sources ix
   The Four Localities x

Acknowledgements xiii

1. Prologue: Dr. Nathaniel Freeman at the Barnstable Court House 1
2. Bloodshed 9
3. Cruises of the HMS *Falcon*, *Kingfisher*, and *Swan* 17
4. The Plight of Nantucket 35
5. The Vineyard Seacoast Company 53
6. Defense of the Elizabeth Islands 59
7. The Loss of the Elizabeth Islands 71
8. Grey's Raid on Martha's Vineyard 85
9. Falmouth Threatened 99
10. Nantucket Raided 111
11. Joseph Dimmick 119
12. The Refugee Fleet Returns 125
13. Nantucket's Protracted Suffering 137
14. Epilogue 147

References 149

Index 151

About the Author 161

List of Illustrations

Page	Caption	Source
cover	Smart Scurmey.	c
xii	Map of Cape Cod.	j
1	Cape Cod Summer's Day.	l
4	Dr. Nathaniel Freeman.	f
11	Boston in 1776, Looking East toward Noodles Island.	n
14	Boston and its Environs, 1776.	n
17	The Chase.	c
22	Captain John Linzee.	z
23	HMS *Falcon*.	n
32	Cleared for Action.	n
33	Brig Working into Harbor.	n
34	Nantucket. Des Barres Chart of 1776.	h
37	18th Century Sailing Vessels.	n
50	Notice for the Arrest of Dr. Samuel Gelston.	n
53	Smart Scurmey.	c
59	The Elizabeth Islands. Des Barres, 1779.	h
67	Attack on Newport, 1778.	n
71	Shaving Mills in Action.	c
84	Vice Admiral Richard, Lord Howe, R. N.	n
85	Major John André, Adjutant to General Clinton.	a
91	Captain Robert Fanshaw, R. N. c.1770.	n
98	Brig with Wind Abeam.	n
101	Woods Hole from Nobska, Looking West.	p
106	English Raid on Woods Hole, April 1, 1779. Franklin L. Gifford, 1930's.	m
109	Falmouth Militia Repels British Invasion. Franklin L. Gifford, 1930's.	m
111	The Town of Sherburne Harbor in the Island of Nantucket.	y

117	Colonial Trading Sloop.	c
119	Colonial Schooner.	c
123	Brig.	c
125	Sulky Captured by the Privateer *Washington* entering Newberryport under a Prize Crew, January 15, 1776.	n
136	Widow's Walk.	w
145	Flintlock Wall Gun (above); Swivel Gun (below).	c
147	A Sail in the Distance.	l

Foreword

About the Chronology

In the following journal, I have collected documents relating to the events of the American Revolution that took place in the waters south and west of Cape Cod and have placed them in chronological order. The ambiguous title *A Journal of Occurrences Along the Rebel Coast – A Chronology of Revolutionary War Naval Events in the Waters South and West of Cape Cod. (1775-1781)*, reflects the dispassionate treatment given to both the Patriot and Loyalist perspectives. Indeed, despite our national pride in the American Revolution and the enlightened principles of our Declaration of Independence, Constitution and Bill of Rights, I cannot help but view the Revolutionary War events experienced by people on the Cape and Islands (and perhaps elsewhere) as anything other than a terrible tragedy – a tragic conflict between two essentially "good" ideologies and worse, a bitter, neighbor-against-neighbor civil war. So bitter and so tragic a history that it may have been convenient to simply forget about it. So it is, perhaps, that the history of local events during the American Revolution are only dimly and possibly inaccurately remembered.

I became amazed by the story of the Revolution particularly if one views the events that occurred on the Elizabeth Islands, Martha's Vineyard, Nantucket, and Falmouth as a single story. What emerges is a cruel dichotomy: The Elizabeth Islands, Martha's Vineyard and Nantucket are of immense importance to the British and, because of their isolation, are forced into neutrality; while Falmouth, of modest strategic value to the British, is able to fend off periodic attacks and retain its enthusiastic Patriotic stance because—as a part of the main—its defense could be quickly reinforced by other Cape militias, notably that of Sandwich.

Sources

The idea of collecting first-hand accounts and ordering them into what might be called a "found" novel—that is, a novel made up of narratives written by people living at the time of the Revolution—it occurred to me after I stumbled on the remarkable resource, *Naval Documents of the American Revolution*. Up until

March 31, 1778, the last entry of Volume 11, most of the entries in this chronology were taken from that source. I used optical character recognition (OCR) software to copy the entries, and most of the graphic images were also scanned from that source. After 1778, Emerson's *The Early History of Naushon* took over; and finally, Starbuck's *The History of Nantucket* furnished much of the last part of the narrative. Freeman's *The History of Cape Cod* was used extensively throughout. So almost everything was copied from these four sources. André's *Journal* furnished the narrative for Grey's Raid in 1778. Internet resources such as The On-Line Institute for Advanced Loyalist Studies, www.royal provincial.com/index.htm, furnished most of the materials on Leonard and Winslow and the Refugee Fleet.

I did not deviate from a strict chronology. The fourteen chapters seemed to me a logical and inevitable parsing of the events into episodes. I did occasionally add items that have no date just to give some relief and a change of pace. Many of these items could have been extended footnotes or appended, but I hoped that their addition to the text would provide a welcome counterpoint.

The Four Localities

What emerges from the *Journal* is that the four localities—Falmouth, the Elizabeth Islands, Martha's Vineyard and Nantucket—each played different but important roles in events.

The Elizabeth Islands had sheep but very few people. The British were at first under siege in Boston and later in Newport and had to scrounge for food for their troops. Naushon was their first supermarket (the Vineyard their second). They were willing to buy but would take the sheep if resisted. Finally Naushon was emptied of people and sheep despite the worthy attempts of the Falmouth militia to protect it. Nashawena (Slocum's Island) and perhaps other of the Elizabeth Islands were Loyalist.

Prior to the Revolution, it seems to me that Nantucket was the Venice of New England. In 1790, Sherburne (Nantucket) was still the fifteenth largest town or city in the United States. As such it suffered terribly at the hands of the British, Loyalist Privateers, and the Continentals. I became deeply sympathetic with the terrible plight of the pacifist-Quaker people of Nantucket: Nantucket was marauded from the beginning to the end of the events chronicled. Whether it was on the balance Patriot, Neutral, or Loyalist is not entirely clear. It may have been all of the above.

Martha's Vineyard was a survivor. It played both sides rather well: It had no choice. At first it was involved in local privateering of British shipping, but later it was entirely subdued by Grey's raid and, as a consequence, ultimately forced to cooperate with George Leonard of the Refugee Fleet to supply Newport with wood and food. Most of the men of the Vineyard were seamen and consequently away at sea.

Falmouth's location and geography, particularly its proximity to the Elizabeth Islands and its defensible position on the mainland, led to Falmouth being the major Patriot stronghold on the Cape's south coast and the singular military and political "muscle" to try to enforce the will of the Patriots on the outlying islands. Barnstable and Wareham chose to be neutral. Like the islands, Provincetown and Chatham were neutral by reason of being exposed and indefensible.

Fred Lawrence, Waquoit, MA, February 2008

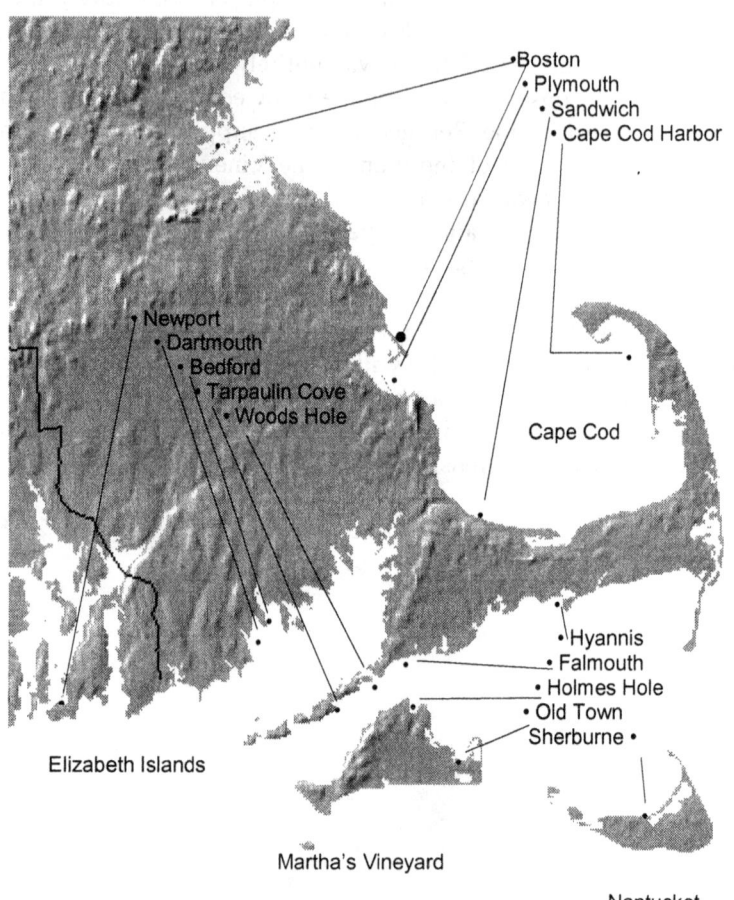

Cape Cod, Martha's Vineyard, and Nantucket. Locations which figure prominently in the Journal are indicated. Buzzard's Bay lies between the Elizabeth Islands and the main, Vineyard Sound lies between the Elizabeth Islands and Martha's Vineyard, Nantucket Sound lies between Nantucket and Cape Cod.

Acknowledgements

Many thanks to Ms. Carolyn Powers and Ms. Mary Sicchio of the Falmouth Historical Society, to Ms. Jennifer Gaines of the Woods Hole Historical Collection and to the Woods Hole Public Library for supplying several key images, for suggesting sources of information for this study, and for their generous help and encouragement. Thanks also to my brother Macy W. Lawrence of PhotoArk Digital Archiving for photographing and enhancing several images. Ms. Roxanne Carlson was of great assistance in editing the document and preparing it for publication.

Cape Cod Summer's Day.

1

Prologue: Dr. Nathaniel Freeman at the Barnstable Court House

September 26, 1774, Barnstable, Massachusetts

Abraham Holmes Memoirs
Rochester, Massachusetts (1834)

...The British Parliament, in its mad career, had assumed a right to mutilate the charter of Massachusetts, which was a solemn *contract* between the KING on the one part, and the PROVINCE on the other. Parliament was not a party to it; nor was it made under any authority from them, or with any reference to 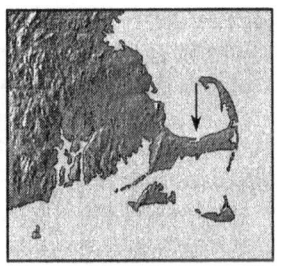 them; and with it they had no more right to interfere than had the Bonzes of Japan: but this authority Parliament assumed, and by an Act had taken from the House of Representatives the right to choose the Council — a right granted the province by its charter; and had authorized the king to appoint the Council by *mandamus*, and directed the *sheriffs* of the several counties to appoint the jurors instead of their being drawn as was provided by law, from the jury box, by the selectmen.

This gave universal alarm, and involved the great body of the people in the most perplexing agitation. They were not insensible of the dangers attending opposition, and yet could not for a moment endure the idea of submitting to so notorious a violation of their rights. After viewing the matter in all its aspects, they agreed that nothing that might follow could be so bad as tame submission; and determined, therefore, to apply a remedy. And as the Court of Common Pleas was to be holden in Barnstable on the first Tuesday in September, it was resolved to begin first with that court, and prevent its sitting for the transaction of any business whatever.

Accordingly [on September 26, 1774] a considerable body of men from Middleboro, more from Rochester, and many from Wareham, repaired to Sandwich on the Monday preceding the time for the opening of the court, and were there joined by a large part of the population of that town. The later part of the day, and the evening, were spent in organizing the body and establishing rules and regulations. Dr. NATHANIEL FREEMAN of Sandwich was unanimously chosen the conductor-in-chief of the enterprise, and officers of lower grade were appointed. FREEMAN, afterwards a brigadier general, was a fine figure of a man, between thirty and forty years of age. He had a well-made face, a florid countenance, a bright and dignified eye, a clear and majestic voice; and wore a handsome black lapelled coat, a tied wig as white as snow, a set-up hat with the point a little to the right; in short, had the very appearance of *fortitude personified*.

On Tuesday morning, the body marched to Barnstable, and were there joined by a considerable portion of the population of that town; making in the whole, as was estimated, about 1500. They took possession of the grounds in front of the court house, in a condensed solid body; and the conductor took his stand on the steps of the court house door.

Commissioners were then appointed to ferret out the disaffected among the people and bring them to a renouncement, in writing, of their "*Toryism*"; and it was ordered that if any should refuse they be brought before the body of the people assembled. The result was, all signed "recantations," though some did it very reluctantly. At length the court made its appearance led on by the high sheriff with a broad cockade on his hat, a long white staff in his left hand and a drawn sword in his right; and the court (OTIS, WINSLOW, and BACON), as the body did not give way, halted about an arm's length from the compact assemblage.

Col. OTIS, the chief justice, a very venerable-looking old gentleman, then addressing the people, inquired, "Gentlemen, what is the purpose for which this vast assemblage is collected here?" and was answered by Dr. Freeman, standing on the steps of the court house, in a loud and clear voice, (for he was at some distance from where the court stood, - "May it please your honor, oppressed by a view of the dangers with which we are surrounded, and terrified by the horribly black cloud which is suspended over our heads and ready to burst upon us,—our safety, all that is dear to us, and the welfare of unborn millions, have directed this movement to *prevent the court from being opened or doing any business*. We have taken all the consequences into consideration; we have weighed them well, and have formed this RESOLUTION which we *shall not rescind*."

The chief justice, then, calmly but firmly replied, "This is a legal and a constitutional court: it has suffered no mutations; the juries have been drawn from the boxes as the law directs; and why would you interrupt its proceedings?—why do you make a leap before you get to the hedge?"

Dr. Freeman responded, "*All this* has been considered. We do not appear here out of any disrespect to this honorable court; nor do we apprehend that if you proceed to business, you will do any thing that we could censure. But, sir, from all the *decisions* of this court, of more than forty shillings amount, an appeal lies; an appeal to what?—to a court holding office during the king's pleasure; a court over which we have no control or influence; a court paid out of the revenue that is *extorted* from us by the illegal and *unconstitutional* edict of foreign despotism; and there the jury will be appointed by the *sheriff*. For this reason, we have adopted this method of stopping the avenue through which business may otherwise pass to that tribunal,—well knowing that if they have no business, they can do us no harm."

The chief justice then said, "As is my duty, I now, in his majesty's name, order you *immediately to disperse* and give the court the opportunity to perform the business of the county."

Dr. Freeman replied, "We thank your honor for having done YOUR duty; WE SHALL CONTINUE TO PERFORM OURS." The court then turned and repaired to the house where they had put up.

Dr. Nathaniel Freeman.

A committee was then chosen, of which Dr. Freeman was the chairman, to wait on the chief justice, in the name of the assemblage, and request him to attend at Boston at the time appointed by the governor for the meeting of a new General Court; and then and there to demand his seat at the Council Board, the chief justice being one of those chosen that year agreeably with the provision of the charter. The chief justice answered, in writing; he thanked them for putting him in mind of his duty; said he had considered the subject, and had concluded to attend and demand his seat, although he did not expect the demand would be successful. The governor, as is known, issued, for some reason, before the time of meeting, another proclamation *forbidding* the members of the General Court to meet. I thought then, and I still continue of the same mind, that I never had seen, nor have I since seen, any man whatever that felt quite so cleverly and happy as did Dr. Freeman during the whole of this business;

and I think no man was ever better qualified to preside on such an occasion. Dr. Freeman, after the conclusion of the business thus far, resigned his post; and, at his recommendation, Major Otis, the clerk of the court, and son of the chief justice, was appointed his successor. The rest of the day was occupied in receiving the recantations of the disaffected, and in raising a *liberty pole*.

The next day the assemblage from the towns above, returned to Sandwich, where they found that the disaffected had committed some outrages. The liberty pole in Sandwich had been cut down, and other offensive acts perpetrated; which things caused some little trouble. The perpetrators were soon arrested and brought *coram nobis*, who, after receiving a severe reprimand and paying the just value of the liberty pole, signing recantations, &c., were liberated.

This was the FIRST ACT OF THE KIND; and, I believe, there was never a Court of Common Pleas held under the king's authority after this time, in the Province; except in the town of Boston, where Gov. Gage, with his troops, had it in his power to control. (f.I-425)[1]

Town Life in the Revolution
William Root Bliss
Wareham, Massachusetts (1889)

...A few months later a lawless event in their neighborhood brought to the notice of the Wareham farmers the disturbed condition of public affairs. A large number of young men met in the adjoining town of Rochester, September 26, 1774, and organized themselves "to make an excursion into the county of Barnstable," and there by forcible means to prevent the Inferior Court of Common Pleas from holding its regular session. This was

---

[1] The code at the end of the narrative gives the source, volume and page number from which it has been copied e.g. f.I-425 stands for <Freeman>, <volume I>, <Page 425>. See References for meaning of the letter code indicating the reference.

one of the oldest courts in the province; its jurymen were selected in town meeting; from its decisions an appeal could be taken to the Superior Court of Judicature in which jurors were drawn by the sheriff. Political agitators declared that the method of drawing jurors by a sheriff, instead of drawing them "out of the box" in town meeting, put in jeopardy the rights of the people! By breaking up the county court it was intended to destroy an avenue through which business could pass to the higher tribunal.

This band of young men, intent on disorder, styled itself "The Body of the People," a title which recalls the three tailors of Tooley Street, who in an address to Parliament styled themselves, "We the People of England." It passed through Wareham, where it was joined by Noah Fearing, John Gibbs, Nathan Briggs, and Salathiel Bumpus, and arrived at Sandwich in the same evening. The next morning it marched to Barnstable, a part on foot, a part on horseback, a drum corps at its head, and Wareham men or boys riding as guards in its rear.

On arriving at Barnstable the band was increased to a large mob, which took possession of the grounds in front of the courthouse and sent scouts through the town to ferret out loyal people and compel them to renounce *"Toryism."* The justices, who were dining together, were notified that the "Body of the People" desired them not to open the court and would send them an order to that effect in writing. These worthy men received the order, and soon appeared in the street, wearing their official robes, and led by the high sheriff, on their way to the court-house to discharge their duties. As the mob did not make way, the chief justice asked for what purpose they were assembled. The leader of the mob, standing on the court-house steps, replied, in the style of a modern politician, "All that is dear to us and the welfare of unborn millions direct us to prevent the court from being opened." To this the chief justice answered,—according to the report written by a Rochester boy named Abraham Holmes, who was one of the mob,—"This is a constitutional court, the jurors have been drawn from the boxes as the law directs, why do you interrupt us? "

The leader then justified himself by the reply: "But from the decisions of this court an appeal lies to a court whose judges hold office during the King's pleasure, over which we have no control!"

Prologue: Dr. Nathaniel Freeman

The mob prevented the session of the court and compelled the justices to sign certain political obligations in harmony with its own views. It was not dispersed until it had made a general disturbance in the town, had resolved to boycott British goods, and to suppress peddlers who sold Bohea tea. (b.176)

2
Bloodshed

April 19, 1775, Boston

Diary of Lieutenant John Barker

Last night between 10 and 11 o'clock all the Grenadiers and Light Infantry of the Army making about 600 Men (under the command of Lt. Coll. Smith of the 10th and Major Pitcairn of the Marines) embarked and were landed upon the opposite shore on Cambridge Marsh; few but the Commandg. Officers knew what expedition we were going upon. 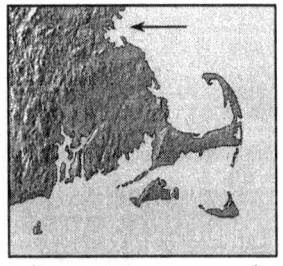 After getting over the Marsh where we were wet up to the knees, we were halted in a dirty road and stood there 'till two o'clock in the morning waiting for provisions to be brought from the boats and to be divided, and which most of the Men threw away, having carried some with 'em.

At 2 o'clock we began our March by wading through a very long ford up to our Middles: after going a few miles we took 3 or 4 People who were going off to give intelligence; about 5 miles on this side of a Town called Lexington which lay in our road...we waited a considerable time there and at length proceeded on our way to Concord, which we then learnt was our destination, in order to destroy a Magazine of Stores collected there.... We march'd into the Town after taking possession of a Hill with a Liberty Pole on it and a flag flying which was cut down; the Yankies had that Hill but left it to us; we expected they wou'd have made a stand there, but they did not chuse it....

Having done the business we were sent upon, We set out upon our return; before the whole had quitted the Town we were fired on from Houses and behind Trees, and before we had gone 1/2 a mile we were fired on from all sides, but mostly from the Rear, where People had hid themselves in houses 'till we had passed and then fired; the Country was an amazing strong one, full of Hills, Woods, stone Walls, &c., which the Rebels did not fail to take advantage of, for they were all lined with People who kept an incessant fire upon us, as we did too upon them but not with the same advantage, for they were so concealed there was hardly any seeing them: in this way we marched between 9 and 10 miles, their numbers increasing from all parts, while ours was reducing by deaths, wounds and fatigue, and we were totally surrounded with such an incessant fire as it's impossible to conceive, our ammunition was likewise near expended....

When we got to Menotomy [Arlington] there was a very heavy fire; after that we took the short cut into the Charles Town road, very luckily for us too, for the Rebels thinking we shou'd endeavour to return by Cambridge had broken down the Bridge and had a great number of Men to line the road and to receive us there; however we threw them and went on to Charles Town without any great interruption. We got there between 7 and 8 o'clock at night, took possession of the hill above the Town and waited for the Boats to carry us over which came some time after; the Rebels did not chuse to follow us to the Hill as they must have fought us on open ground and that they did not like....

We embarked and got home very late in the night. Thus ended this Expedition, which from beginning to end was as ill plan'd and ill executed as it was possible to be; had we not idled away three hours on Cambridge Marsh waiting for provisions that were not wanted, we shou'd have had no interruption at Lexington, but by our stay the Country People had got intelligence and time to assemble. We shou'd have reached Concord soon after day break, before they cou'd have heard of us, by which we shou'd have destroyed more Cannon and Stores, which they had had time enough to convey away before our arrival; we might also have got easier back and not been so much harrassed, as they wou'd not have had time to assemble so many People; even the People of Salem and Marblehead above 20 miles off had intelligence and time enough to march and meet us on our return; they met us somewhere about Menotomy but they lost a good many for their pains.

Thus for a few trifling stores the Grenrs. and Lt Infantry had a march of about 50 Miles (going and returning) through an Enemy's Country, and in all human probability must every Man

Boston in 1776, Looking East toward Noodles Island.

have been cut off if the Brigade had not fortunately come to their Assistance; for when the Brigade joined us there were very few Men had any ammunition left, and so fatigued that we cou'd not keep flanking parties out, so that we must soon have laid down our Arms, or been picked off by the Rebels at their pleasure — nearer to — and we not able to keep 'em off. (n.1-199)

Signal for War

Several regiments, we have said, followed Gage soon after his arrival. He had begun to repair the fortifications upon Boston Neck; had seized the ammunition in Charlestown arsenal; and had again been recruiting, so that his forces were 10,000 strong. He now sent out a detachment to take possession of the stores at Salem and Concord. When Gage sent his troops to seize the stores at Concord, the march, though in the night, was discovered; and early in the morning of the 19th, as the troops under Colonel Smith and Major Pitcairn reached Lexington, they found about seventy men of the "minute company" of that town under arms. Pitcairn riding up to them, called out, "Disperse, you rebels!" and not being obeyed at once discharged his pistol and ordered his troops to fire. Eight Americans were killed and others wounded.

It was the intention of the people so to conduct as to place their adversaries in the wrong; determined that if hostilities must commence, England should be the aggressor; but it was equally their determination to repel with firmness the first hostile attack. This is, to say the least, one of the few battles comparatively in which human blood has not been shed in vain. It was truly an occasion on which the blood of patriots proved to be the seed of liberty; the beginning of that sanguinary contest that resulted in the establishment of American independence.

On the return of the troops the people of the neighborhood had very generally gathered in arms, and the retreating troops were attacked in all directions. At Lexington, a British reinforcement came to the rescue and secured the retreat of the red-coats to Boston, after the damage of 60 killed and 180 wounded. The American loss was 50 killed and 34 wounded. (f.I-471)

Letter of W. Watson to N. Freeman
Plymouth, April 24, 1775

Dear Col. Freeman,

I congratulate you and our good friends in Sandwich on the grandest event that ever took place in America: I mean the late battle Concord, &c. That 700 poor, despised Yankees (1 glory in the name) should have put to flight and totally defeated 1700 of Lord North's best picked troops, consisting of grenadiers and Earl Percy's regiment of Welsh Fusiliers, is a circumstance deeply mortifying to those who thought themselves invincible.

One of our Kingston friends was in Boston when the vanquished troops returned, and was at the ferry when they were brought over, who says he cannot express the mortification, disappointment and chagrin that appeared in their countenances. Cartloads of the wounded were hurried to the hospital (many of whom are since dead), their mouths belching out curses and execrations.

We have disarmed our Tories, and they are in a melancholy situation—suing and begging for reconciliation on any terms. We are in high spirits, and don't think it is in the power of all Europe to subjugate us; for it is evident that the Lord of Hosts has declared in our favor, and to this God let us ascribe all the glory and all the praise. The poor, wicked, *mandamus* party are fled to the ships; and to what can they fly next? I am sure they have not a good conscience to flee to.

I wish them future happiness; but I cannot in conscience wish them much good in this life. I sincerely wish and most heartily pray that a proper sense of this very remarkable interposition of Providence in our favor may have a proper effect on the minds of a much injured and greatly insulted people. Ned Winslow was in the action, and had his horse shot under him....

I am, sir, with much esteem, and most sincere affection, Your humble servant, in great haste,   W. WATSON. (f.I-471)

Boston and its Environs, 1776.

April 30, 1775, Boston Harbor

Vice Admiral Samuel Graves
to Captain John Linzee, H.M.S. *Falcon*

Whereas in the present Rebellious State of this Country it is extremely difficult to procure fresh Meat even for the sick of his Majs Squadron under my command, and whereas I am informed there is a great quantity of Cattle upon the Elizabeth Islands near Falmouth in this Province, which it is absolutely necessary to prevent being carried to the Main; You are hereby required and directed with all possible Dispatch to proceed to Tarpawlin Cove in his Majs Sloop under your Command and there endeavour to hinder any Cattle live Stock or Hay upon the Islands being taken off, but you are upon no Account to suffer any Injury to be done to the Property or the Persons of the Inhabitants by any persons whatsoever, so long as they shall demean themselves like dutiful and peaceable Subjects to his Majesty and if by any means you can prevail upon the Owners of the Cattle to dispose of them for his Majesty's Use, you are to acquaint me thereof as soon as possible as to the Terms upon which they are inclined to sell.

And as you cannot remain in Tarpawlin Cove without great Danger when the Wind is Easterly, you are to move occasionally to Holmes Hole [Vineyard Haven] and Mannantha [Menemsha] Bite as the Easterly or Southerly Winds shall render necessary. For all other Orders I refer you to my general Orders and Instructions which you have already received.

Given under my Hand on Board His Majs Ship *Preston* at Boston the 30th April 1775 By Command of the Admiral G. Gefferina.

Sam Graves (n.1-252)

**Vice Admiral Samuel Graves
to Captain John Linzee, H.M.S.** *Falcon*

Notwithstanding my Orders to you of this Morning you are hereby required and directed to proceed as fast as possible to Martha's Vineyard in his Majs Sloop under your Command, where you will find the Ship *Champion*, Paddock Master, laden with Flour and Wheat; You are to seize the said Ship and send her immediately to Boston under the Command of an Officer from the Falcon, and then proceed to Eliza Islands according to my former Orders.

Given under my Hand on board his Majs Ship *Preston* at Boston the 30 April 1775.

Sam Graves (n.1-252)

The Chase.

3

Cruises of the HMS Falcon, Kingfisher, and Swan

May 5, 1775, Bedford, Massachusetts

Extract of a Letter from Newport, Rhode Island Dated May 10 [1775]

Last Friday [May 5] the *Falcon*, Captain [John] Lindsey [Linzee], took two sloops at Bedford [New Bedford], with intention of sending them to the Islands near the Vineyard, to carry from thence a parcel of sheep to Boston. The Bedford people resented this conduct in such a manner as to immediately fit out two

sloops, with thirty men on board, and last Saturday [May 6] retook them both, with fifteen men on board. In the action there were three of the men of war sailors badly wounded, one of whom is since dead. The other thirteen they immediately sent to Taunton Jail. (n.1-303)

Massachusetts Spy, Wednesday, May 24, 1775
Worcester, Massachusetts

The week before last, the *Falcon* sloop of war, was cruising about Cape Cod, and meeting with a wood sloop, in ballast, seized her, but promising the Skipper to release him and his vessel if he would give information of any vessel that was just arrived from the West-Indies with a cargo on board, he at length told the Captain of the *Falcon* that there was a sloop at Dartmouth, which had just arrived; whereupon the Captain of the *Falcon*, instead of releasing the wood sloop, armed and manned her, and sent her in search of the West-Indiaman; they found the vessel lying at anchor, but her cargo was landed; however, they seized her and carried her off after putting part of their crew and some guns and ammunition on board.

Notice of this getting on shore, the people fitted out a third sloop, with about thirty men and two swivel guns, and went in pursuit of these royal pirates, whom they come up with at Martha's Vineyard, where they lay at anchor at about a league's distance from each other; the first surrendered without firing a gun, our people after putting a number of hands on board, bore down upon the other, which by this time had got under sail, but the people in the Dartmouth sloop coming up with her, the pirates fired upon them; the fire was immediately returned, by which three of the pirates were wounded, among whom was the commanding officer; our people boarded her immediately, and having taken both sloops, carried them into Dartmouth, and sent the prisoners to Cambridge, from whence nine of them were yesterday brought to this Town. (n.1-515)

Nathaniel Freeman to the Massachusetts Provincial Congress
Sandwich, Massachusetts, May 29, 1775

Honble Gentlemen:

In consequence of Complaint made to the Committee of correspondence of the Town of Sandwich by Messrs Simeon Wing and Jesse Barlow we have thought it advisable to represent to your Honours the circumstances of their Vessels being taken by Capt [John] Linsey of the *Falcon* & retaken by a Schooner from Dartmouth under command of Capt [Daniel] Egery, and to beg some advice and order of the Congress may be passed concerning it.

Mr. Wing's Vessel commanded by his Son Thomas Wing has been ply'd as a wood Boat to carry wood to Nantucket from Sandwich [now Bourne] for some years past and it hath been the usual practice for them to settle with the Custom House once a year the Officer of whom always gave them their Choice of paying twelve pence pr tripp or the whole at the years end and this hath been we find up[on] examining the Common practice with other vessels who have followed the same business at the same place —

Upon Capt Wings returning from Nantucket through the Vineyard Sound, His Sloop was taken by a Barge from sd Capt Lindsey. An indian Fellow on board of Wing informd Capt Lindsey of sd Barlows Vessel which had run in Cargo lately from the West Indies and was laden with Provisions in Buzzards Bay Bound thither again as he said. Capt Lindsey employed Capt Wings vessel putting 14 men on board to proceed up the Bay and take sd Barlows vessel which they carried off. The master of this latter Vessel was taken with Wing being then on Board as a passenger, so that both vessels with all the Crew passengers &c were taken & proceeding to the Cove to Capt Lindsey —

Mr. Barlow made application to some people at Dartmouth who went with a Sloop one half of which Barlow ventured & took both Vessels and men with their arms &c and carried them into Dartmouth. Messrs Wing & Barlow applyd to the Dartmouth People who took the vessels for them again the People offer'd them their vessels upon Wing paying them Eight Dollars and Barlows paying 10 Dollars, with which they complyd & Wing paid the money after which the Dartmouth people detained the Vessels till the Orders of Congress could be known, and now refuse to deliver up sd Vessels without Wing & Barlows paying 45 Dollars and giving Bond of a very extraordinary nature to indemnify sd Dartmouth People &c.

These are a true state of facts as nearly as we after examination of sd Wing & Barlow can ascertain, and the sd Wing & Barlow thinking they ought to have their Vessels again without further difficulty desire the Committee of Correspondence of this town to lay the matter before you and pray your Orders hereon to which they profess their readiness to submit to & acquiesce in. We are your Honours [&c] the Committee of Sandwich.

Signed Nathl Freeman pr Order (n.1-558)

May 5, 1775, Tarpaulin Cove

Deposition of Elisha Nye
[Barnstable, Massachusetts] May 31, 1775

I, Elisha Nye, Inholder Living on one of the Elizabeth Islands, Comm Called Naushan, and near to Tarpalan Cove, Testafieth and saith, that Time about the 5th of May, the Sloop of War called the Faulkland [*Falcon*] Command'd by Capt. [John] Linzey, came into the Cove, and as soon as the Vessel had come to Anchor, the Captain came on Shore with his Boat's Crew all Armed, and came to the House and Said unto the Deponent "you need not be Scard"; upon which he told him it was Enough to Scare any Body to see so many Men come on Shore Armed; And the Women are all Fled and to where he knew not; upon which Capt Linzey told Him to call them in, for he did not mean to hurt any Body — upon which Promise, I & my Family were Satisfyed;

Soon after that the Captain asked to walk with him; which he Comply'd with; and in the Course of the walk, he demanded to know what Stock I had, and Added to tell him Right, for if he did not, he would take all that he met; upon which I gave him the Account.

Then the Captain told me, the Deponent, if I sold anyone of them he would take the Remainder by force; upon which I told him, if he were here when they were fit for market he might have them, paying the Price I used to have. Soon after, he went to Rhode Island.... (n.1-576)

May 6, 1775, Newport
Diary of Dr. Ezra Stiles

This day another Man o'War Capt. Lindley came here, so we have now three ships here—tho' it is said that the *Rose* Man o'War Capt. [James] Wallace is called away. (n.1-291)

May 7, 1775, Robinson's Hole
Statement of Daniel Egry
May 10, 1775

Daniel Egry of Dartmouth Says that last Sabbath [May 7] a whale Man went thro' Robinson's hold [hole], into the Sound Just at the Eastward lay 3 Tenders, who fired upon the Schooner the Master then ordered the Schooner about again & run into the hold, all the People then left the Vessel by the Masters orders the officer of a Barge then came on board and snapt his Pistol at the Master, which did not go off tho' well primed & all the rest of the Barge Crew cock't their pistols but were ordered by the Officer not to fire—

The People of the 3 tenders swore they would have all the Stock on the Island, having forced the Tenants to give an Inventory thereof & intended to seize five vessels to carry them off & pursued one Vessel which hove in sight—the Name of the Island is Nashon & owned by Mr. [James] Bowdoin suppose there is 3000 Sheep on the Island & a large Stock of Cattle it is supposed they intended to rob the several Islands near in which Islands it is supposed there was 10,000 Sheep beside Cattle. (n.1-303)

Captain John Linzee.

May 11, 1775, Holmes Hole

Journal of His Majesty's Sloop *Falcon*
John Linzee, Commanding
May 1775 Thursdy 11

At Single Anchor in Holmes's Hole. At 7 [AM] Came too Et Chop Holmes's Hole W B S old Town S Bespoke a Ship from Maryland to Cork laden with flower and Corn which we detain Sent the Master and 6 Men on Bd the above Ship 2 Came too in Holmes's Hole with the Bt Br East Chop Et Wt Chop SW at 11 Brought too a Schooner from Boston. At 3 P M Brot too a Sloop at 6 Seizd a Sloop from Nantuckett for Having no Clearance. (n.1-311)

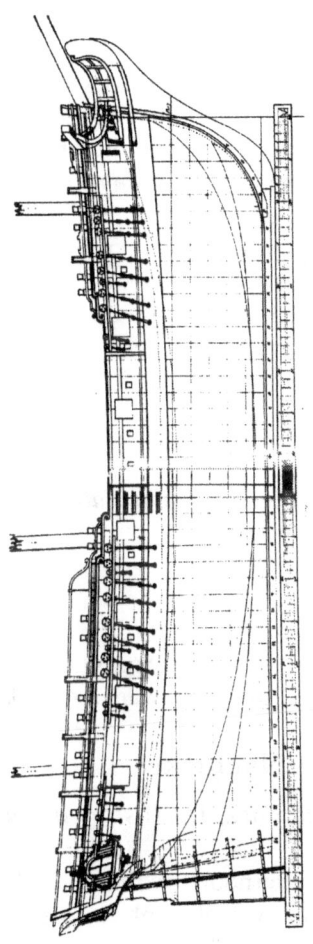

HMS Falcon.

May 12, 1775, Holmes Hole

Journal of His Majestys Sloop *Falcon*
John Linzee, Commanding
May 1775 Frydy 12

Att Single Anchor in Holmes's Hole. At 10.A M Sent the Gunners Mate Surgeons mate and 11 Men On Board the above Sloop [seized the previous day] At ½ past 11 Weighd and Came to Sail at 2 PM fird a Six poundr and a Swivel Shotted to bring too a Schooner at 4 Came too in Tarpolen Cove with the Bt Br Wt point SW. At 9 fird a Six poundr and Swivel at a Schooner. (n.1-322)

May 22, 1775, Tarpaulin Cove

Journal of His Majestys Sloop *Falcon*
John Linzee, Commanding
May 1775 Tuesdy 22d

In Tarpolean Cove. AM at 7 fird two Swivels & two Six Pounders Shotted and Brat too a Brigg from Dominica. 2 PM Deserted two Marines and the Pursers Steward. (n.1-503)

May 23, 1775, Nantucket

Extract from Starbuck, *The History of Nantucket* **(1924)**

...Late in the afternoon of the 23d of May a small vessel entered the [Nantucket] harbor carrying about a hundred Provincial soldiers, who landed at the wharf and marched up into the Town. It was reported that they were after a quantity of flour shipped to the Island sometime before, and which it  was further reported was threatened with seizure by the troops under Gen. Gage. They [Capt. Joshua Davis et al.] remained on the

Island until May 27th, quartered in stores, then departed, carrying with them between fifty and sixty whale-boats. This expedition was apparently not ordered by the Provincial Council and was undertaken on the initiative of Joshua Davis. (s.182)

May 25, 1775, Tarpaulin Cove

Journal of His Majesty's Sloop *Falcon*
John Linzee, Commanding
May 1775 Thursdy 25

Att Single Anchor in Tarpolean Cove. At 6 P M fird two Six pounders Shotted and Brot too a Schooner from St. Vincents. (n.1-526)

May 26, 1775, Tarpaulin Cove

Deposition of Elisha Nye
[Barnstable, Massachusetts] May 31, 1775

...On the 26th Instant a Sloop came into the Cove, with about Twenty Passengers, Men, Women, & Children in great Distress for Provisions, and made application to me for Supplyes. Capt Linzey knowing that, (his Boat having boarded her) sent his Boat on Shore, and forbid my letting them have any. Than I advised them to apply to Capt Linzey, and see if they could not prevail upon him to let them have some; accordingly they went; Afterwards the Captain of the Sloop told me, that he absolutely Refused them, and said "Damn the Dog that would let them have any; and if they were not gone immediately, he would Sink them," upon which, they set sail Immediately without any Supplyes —

And further, the Deponent Declareth, that the Doctor came on shore, and said that the Captain's Orders were, that I should go with him, the said Doctor, and Destroy all the Boats belonging to the Island. I told him I could not go upon such Business as that; he said he would send me on board the Ship if I did not go; upon which I found I must Comply, and Accordingly went with him, and saw him, the Doctor, Stave three Boats. (n.1-576)

May 29, 1775, Tarpaulin Cove

Deposition of Elisha Nye
[Barnstable, Massachusetts] May 31, 1775

...On the 29th, about Eight o'Clock in the Evening Lo, the said Doctor came on Shore, and told me he had come for my Sheep, upon which, I told him they were out in the Pasture and I could not get them into the pen it being Dark, but would fetch them in as Early in the Morning as he pleased –

The Answer from the Doctor was, "Damn you! what did you turn them out for?"

The Reason, I told him, was, that they [the ministerial forces] had got out [obtained] their own Sheep, and did not say any thing more about when they should want mine, and I thought it best the Sheep should be let out to feed; upon which, the said Doctr said to me, "Damn you! go on Board the Ship and I'll see what they were turn'd out for."

I told him I would not, but would go and try to get the Sheep up: he said "Well, Damn you! make haste!" and Swang his Sword over my head.

But upon Trial I found it so Dark I could not get them in; but, on my Return, was Inform'd that he, the Doctor had sent onboard for more help to Carry me & my Brother on board the Ship; upon which, with the Abuses & threats I had Received before, I thought it Time to make my Escape, which I did, to the main land and begged the Assistance of the People, who Readily came to my Assistance. —

When I Return'd, which was about three o'Clock in the Morning, Some of my Family told me, they had been on shore, armed, and taken all my Calves, being Seven in Number; two of the poorest & Smalest, they sent on shore in the Morning, the Others, with four Sheep they had some days before; they carried them off without paying any thing for them.

I do further Declare the Abuses and threats I Received from Capt Linzey & the Doctor were the Occasion of my Moving off the Island, leaving my Interest, and I Declare that I never Refused Capt Linzey or any other person Belonging to any ship of war, Entertainment in my House or Supply of Provisions that I had on my farm that I could Spare and I further Declare that on the night of the 29th instant afforesaid [the] Doctor (as my wife Informs me) Came on Shore and Demanded my gun with his Sword in hand which she Delivered to him and I have not Seen it Since tho the only weapon of Defence that I had on the Island: the value of the Sheep Calves and Gun which they took frome me and the use of my Horse and well are as follows, viz: —

	Lawfull Money
Four sheep value	£ 2-16-0
3 Calves four Month old	£ 3- 6-0
3 Calves two Months old	£ 2- 8-0
4 Quarters of veal, weight 60 pounds Sold before and delivered	£ 0-16-0
One Gun, taken out of my House by the Doctor of the Ship of great value	£ 3-0-0
Riding my Horse and use of my Well	£ 3-0-0
[Total]	£ 15- 6-0

(n.1-576)

Affidavit of John Tucker and Others
Barnstable, Massachusetts, May 31, 1775

We the Subscribers Testify and Say, that on the 29th day of May 1775 Captain [John] Linsey Commander of a Ship of war then at Tarpaulin Cove Came with a Number of armed men and landed on one of the Elizabeth Islands called Reskatemeth and came to the place where the men that oned part of the Stock on Said Island were Sheering their Sheep and demanded the Sheep Saying and promising that he would pay for them and give the full value of the Sheep or words to that purpose. But the owners of Said Sheep told him that they were unwilling to part with them, but if he would take them, they Should not molest him as most of the owners of the Sheep were of the people Called Quakers and that they would not be concerned in Defending themselves or their Interest by force of Armes but would treat him with civility. But Said Capten with his men took Said Sheep and Carried them away, Some Shorn and many not Shorn: the Sheep were hurried away in Such a manner that we Could not take an account of the number with exactness but according to the best of our judgment the numbers and value of the Sheep are as follows. viz —

	Lawful money
Took from Joseph Tucker and Sons 93 Sheep, value	£68 - 8[s] - 0[d]
Took from Jeremiah Robinson 17 Sheep, value	£12 - 4[s] - 0[d]
Took from William & Elisha Robinson 24 Sheep, value	£ 14 - 8[s] - 0[d]
Took from Ebenezer Meiggs 72 Sheep value	£51 - 15[s] - 6[d]

John Tucker
Jeremiah Robinson
Elisha Robinson
Ebenezer Meiggs
(n.1-575)

Stephen Nye to Colonel Nathaniel Freeman
Sandwich [Massachusetts] May 31, 1775

Sir :

I would give you a relation of Capn. [John] Linsey, proceeding at the Islands since your going from here. On Sunday [May 28] he rec'd a reinforcement by a Schooner from Boston, & proceeded from thence to the West End of the Island where they took off about Two Hundred Sheep; chiefly from Tuckers [Pasque] Island which belonged to John Wing from there they came down to the cove & ordered the Sheep there to be yarded which was accordingly done, but it being near Night they concluded to leave them in the Yard until morning.

They really insulted abused & threatened the People for their backwardness in assisting them. In the Night word was brought off to Falmouth of the above proceedings (by [Elisha] Nye who immediately went back to take care of his Family) on which a Number of men well equipt immediately went on the Island; before there arrival at the cove the Sheep were turned out of the Yard into the Woods.

The People from the Ship had been on Shore & on finding the Sheep were gone were still more enraged & took all the arms they could find, 6 Calves, & the Hoggs and carried them off. When the People from Falmouth got to the cove (which was before Day) they Placed themselves in the Bushes & lay undiscovered.

In the morning, the Boat came on Shore with the Doctor Boatswain &c; whom they might have taken had they not expected the Capn. ashore soon, however the Boat soon went back without going to the House & both Vessels immediately weighed Anchor & went Down to Homes' Hole where they lay last Night at Anchor. Capn [Barachiah] Bassett is now on the Island with about 50 Men, & will Tarry to Guard the Stock until we have the advice of the congress what method is best to take.

By the best account there is not less than Four Thousand Sheep & between Two & three Hundred Homed cattle & a Number of Horses in the Island of Naushaun & Perhaps nigh as many on the other Islands. It is generally Judged That Fifty or Sixty Men Placed on the Island at Tarpaulin Cove would Guard the above Stock. It is certainly impracticable to bring it off & it must most certainly either be destroyed where it is or fall into the Hands of our Enemies. Which is best the Congress must Judge. Their Determination we should be Glad of as soon as Possible for we fear the men now there will be impatient to come off unless they are put under Pay.

Capn Bassett is perhaps the best officer that can he placed there His Courage & Conduct have been heretofore well approved, & he is moreover well acquainted with the Ground on the Island which must certainly be of great advantage. There went a Number of men from This Town Some of whom are (we conclude now on the Island). We hope the Congress will let us have there advice & Determination as Soon as Possible and Pray that in all their Determinations they will be Councelled by the Supream Councellor & are Sir [&c.]

Stephen Nye (n.1-578)

June 4, 1775, Plymouth

Joshua Davis to the Committee of Supplies of the Massachusetts Provincial Congress
Plymouth, Sunday Evening 10 o'clock, June 4, 1775

Gentelman I have Jest Recd your order for Some Flower & am Much plesd that I have it in in Kingston to suply But am Sorrey that it is out of My power to give That Assistance in Despaching it to Watertown I should be glad to Having gest Recd Inteligence Half an ouer ago of a Vessel at some part of Bozards Bay 600 Bushls of good Corn 140 bb of 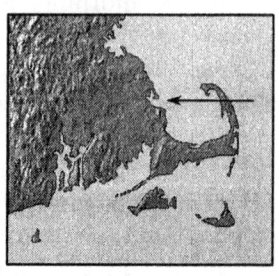 flower 80 bb of pork which Capt Sopers Was so good as to Perswaid over from Nantuckt & had got in safe which is a wonder to me The Sound being so full of Tenders I think it My Duty to Secuer that Cargo in som safe-Plaice from the Ravegors of our Sea & Land. Altho I have no spetial orders for that vessel, shall accordingly go as Sune as Possabal for that purpos & hop to meat with Desierd Suceses.

I Rote you a few Lines yesterday how far I had proseded & which I Belive you have Not Recd but trust you Will Before this Shall Mak it my endevor to git the Rest of the flower and Boats as Sune as posabel to Kingston.

If I am Wrong in Securing the Cargo Mentioned, ples to Impute it to my Ignorance or Zeal for the glores Case & Not to My forwardness In taking in hand what I have no Business with & Shall Be alway Redey to Execute your orders so fare as my abilites or Strengh Extend, I am Genterlmen [&c.]

Joshua David [Davis]

P.S. I shall give all the assistance in Convayin the flower that Time Will permit As Delays are Dangorous Shall Not wait for your orders in Securin the Above sd Cargo. (n.1-610)

August 18, 1775, Tarpaulin Cove

Journal of His Majesty's Sloop *Kingfisher*,
Captain James Montagu, Commanding
August 1775 Friday 18 in Tarpawline Bay

At Day Break Saw A No. of Armed Rebels Abreast the Ship fired 21 Guns to Disperse the Rebels At 4 AM Came to S. 1 PM Empd working into Rhode Isld Harbour. At 3 Anchored wth B.Br in 16 fm. (n.1-1173)

New England Chronicle, Thursday, August 31, 1775
Cambridge, Massachusetts

By a gentleman from Dartmouth, we hear, that a few Days ago, as one of the piratical Ships of war (supposed to be the King-Fisher) was passing up the Sound between Martha's Vineyard and the Elizabeth Islands, she stood into Tarpaulin Cove, close in with one of the Houses, where stood a Number of People without Arms, looking at the Ship; when, without the least Provocation they received a Number of Cannon Balls, and some Musket Shot, from the Ship, which obliged them to secure themselves: After which the Ship fired a Number of Cannon Shot at the House, some of which went through the same, and damaged several Barrels of Provisions &c. but happily no Person was killed or wounded. As soon as this was done, the ship immediately put about and came to Anchor at a considerable Distance from the Shore, and soon after made off. (n.1-1270)

Cleared for Action.

Brig Working into Harbor.

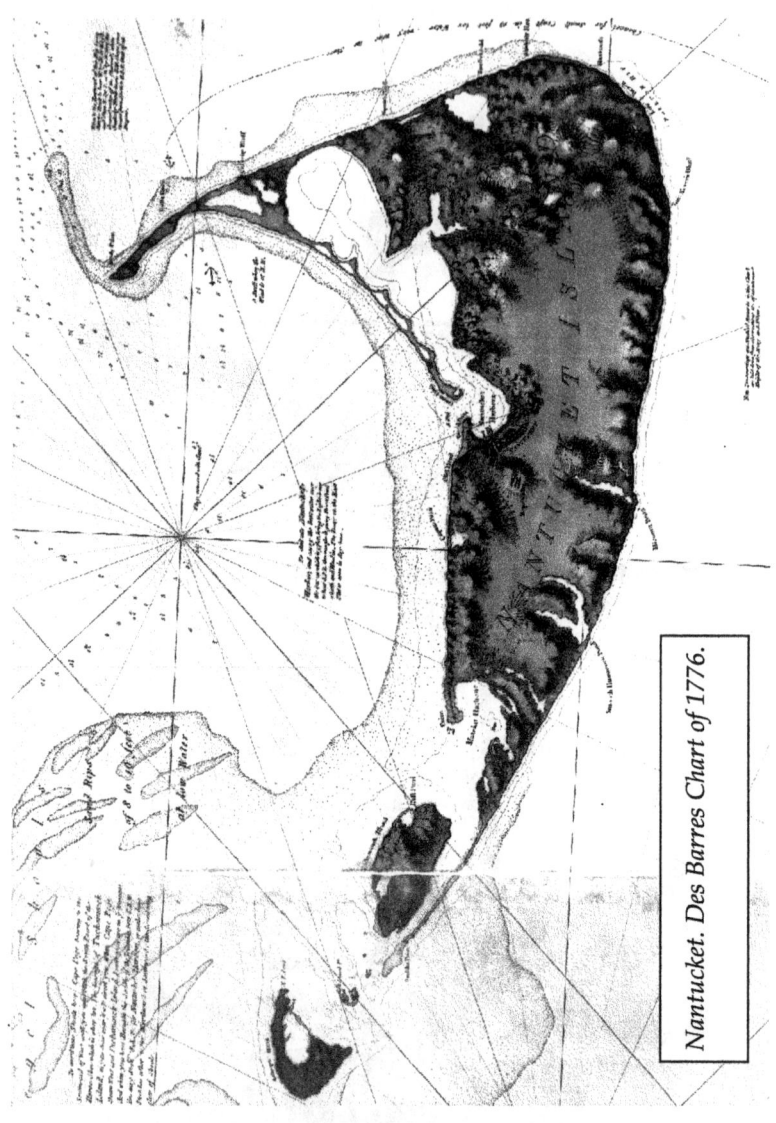

Nantucket. Des Barres Chart of 1776.

4
The Plight of Nantucket

September 1, 1775, Nantucket

Jonathan Jenkins to Dr. Nathaniel Freeman Sr.

Nantucket, 1 Sept 1775

I use the freedom from the former acquaintance I had with your Person, to request the favr of a correspondance by Letters, if the present difficulties have not taken up yr attention so far as to disable you to comply as being upon an Island have Not an Oppy of geting the right of any Story, & you being placed in such a Station as to be knowing to all that transpires; so various are the accots. we have here, that there is no knowing which is right, we have heard that it past a Resolve, that no provision should be brought to this Island & that all communication was to be stopt.

I understand that they censor us as Tory upon the Main, & charge us with supplying [General] Tom Gage with Provisions, it is all fals, there has never been any kind of Provision whatsoever gone from here to Boston, except three Barrels of Flour which Wm Rotch sent as a present to three Widow; which he sent the time that Capt Richd Coffin went down to bring Geyer & Burgess's Ship that was carried there by a King Ship. I must acknowledge that our leading Men, have been very backward in not vindicating the Character of the Island, but let so many false storys pass about & not take notice of it.

As to the inhabitance here being Tory, they are not, but as well wishers to the Cause contending, as any sett of People whersoever, but the Situation of this Island is Such as will not admit of our doing anything except we pack up our all & abandon it, we are no way capable of defending ourselves, from even an Arm Schooner with twenty Soldiers on board, did we not make it evident to Capt [Joshua] Davis when he came on here for Whale boat with his Hundred Men? did we not supply them with all the Powder, ball & Guns that we had, we did & that am knowing too, Several Men whose principles were such as would not admit of there Supplying any person with instruments of War, never objected or shew any dislike when thier Clarks or any other took out of thier Stores powder & Lead to Supply the Soldiers with. What has there been requested of us, that we have not comply'd too? you have never ask'd Men of us, when ever men are Necessary from this Island, I doubt not but we shall be able to turn out a Hundred or More of as good Marksmen as any of the Rifle Men & men who wants not for courrage. It very much surprisd me to hear that that half Starv'd [torn] the best times Baree River should resolve at their Town Meeting Not to Supply us with any of the Necessarys of Life, they never had one tenth part of provision enough to subsist on among themselves, but carried from here the Chief of their support, without us they would all Starve in a heap, since their Resolves there people has been obligd to bring over here all the Cash they could muster to purchase beef Pork flour &c. which they us'd to get by bringing over Homspun Cloath, Stocking, thread &c those that are not able to purchase a barrell of any kind have been about to the Private Houses & beg'd them to Share five or six pound Pork & beef & seven pound flour, Molls Sugar &c in the same manner & acknowledge that if the communication is not soon free again, that many of their poor people will suffer, many whose sole dependance was in bringing over fruit & roots to purchase beef with is now cut of[f] by the rash & inconsiderate resolve what I have freely scrawld upon this Sheet hope you'l not expose to the speculation of any for want of time & my paper falling Short conclude in Subscribing myself your Friend &[c.]

Jona Jenkins (n.1-1283)

October 3, 1775, Nantucket

Diaries of Kezia Coffin
Extract from Starbuck, *The History of Nantucket* **(1924)**

...Sam'l Starbuck came in today from Newport tells that we shall have provisions from the main by First applying to the Falmouth committee & procuring papers. —great Condescension in their high mightinesses.

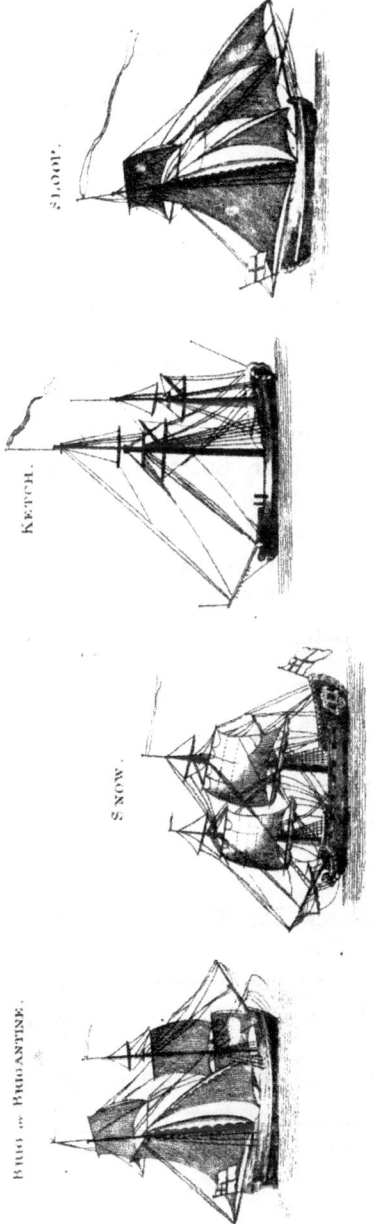

18th Century Sailing Vessels.

October 6, 1775, Nantucket

...Richard Mitchell & Stephen Hussey came to the Island today — have been from this town to the general court to try to get Liberty for us to have necessaries brought here — they have obtained something by going as is mentioned the third of this month.

October 9, 1775, Nantucket

...A few minutes before 12 o'clock Rand and P(hineas) F(anning) came to the Barr, Sailed 8 clock last night from Shelter Island as quick or the quickest passage ever made from there here, they went after provisions. Mr. Fanning petitioned the Committee for leave to bring provisions or wood, but the(y) would suffer him to bring neither any more than to bring him home. They pretended that they believ'd Rand bound to the Enemy — they gave him a permit for so much Beef, Butter, chees, wood &c &c. as they thought would bring them home & put a Committee to see that they took no more in — but by stealth they took more in than they were allowed to. They brought 60 or 70 weight of Butter as much chees, 1 Cow dead, 2 Bbls Cyder, 3 Bushels Quinces — several Bushels Apples dried Cheries, Peas, Apples &c, one deer, skin & all.

October 19, 1775, Nantucket

...Mr. Fanning sailed for Long Island for provisions intending to stop at Falmouth for a permit. (s.192ff)

Extract from Starbuck, *The History of Nantucket* (1924)

To avoid capture and the terrible consequences it involved, the craft in which the people of Nantucket sought to import their food-stuffs were long and narrow, built of frail materials and constructed with special reference to speed. When chased by enemy vessels, they carried such a press of sail that they not infrequently were swamped and their crews perished. (s.207)

September 16, 1775, Holmes Hole

**Extract of a Letter from a Gentleman
Dated Edgartown (Martha's Vineyard), September 18, 1775**

On the 16th Instant, his Majesty's ship *Swan*, Capt. James Ascough [Ayscough], lay at Homes's Hole to Anchor, with a Tender. Said Tender being observed to take on board a number of Marines from the ship, and pursue several boats as they passed, and frequently running backward and forward by the Point of said Harbour, the People suspecting they were on no good Design, kept a Guard with about twelve Men, to watch their Motions; said Tender discovering three Men leaning on a fence near my house, they stood for the shore, as near as they could, and instantly fired two Guns, about 2 pounders, with Grape Shot, which was followed immediately with several volleys of small Arms from the Marines, which put the women and children in great confusion. — Said Guard running direct for the shore, the Tender instantly stood off, and before they could get to the shore by reason of a pond, she was out of shot. Altho' the shot flew very thick, a number of Women and Children escaped without hurt. (n.2-134)

November 16, 1775, Nantucket

Shubael Lovell to Captain James Ayscough, H.M. Sloop *Swan*

Sir:

After my humble respects to you, I am very sorry of the misfortune you met with, as I was informed, by the master of your tender, that you had very much hurt one of your eyes, which I took this opportunity to let you know that I am still a good friend to Government, and to let you know, by writing, that I never have been actor in any things against Government, and have never taken-up any carnal weapons against the King's troops, but have suffered so as to have my gun taken from me, because I have bore my testimony against the measures that the America [party] have taken to get their liberties, as they say they do; and, as I will not take up arms against the King's troops, and to rightly bear the title of a Rebel against my King, I have been threatened of being shot by those that is greatly against Government, yet I never intend to take up arms (through Divine assistance, although I may lose my life), against my King, knowing he has undoubted right to be a terror to evil-doers, and I hope he will be a praise to them that do right.

Captain Ayscough, I shall take it a great favour, and should be humbly obliged to you, if you would inform the Governour and Admiral of me, as it is not a thing impossible for me (by land) to get a letter to Boston, or to come myself, to let them know my mind, without risking my life, and wife and children's lives, and to lose all my estate; and, as you took me and my schooner, about two or three months ago, as I was going into Nantucket, and did use me with great civility, and I did then let you know my mind about the forces, and you did take my name down, and where I lived, which now makes me to take the boldness to trouble you with these few lines, desiring you would oblige me so much as to do all you can for me in these evil times, that if it should please the King's Majesty to show any mercy to any innocent persons, that I might share part with such, as a true King's subject, so that I might save my life and estate, if the King should conquer the America [party]. And I would, also, inform you that I have got a brother, and a cousin, whose name is Daniel Lovell and Christopher Lovell, which, both of them, are good friends to Government, which did desire me, that if I had a chance, to inform some of the King's officers of them.

And now, pray, sir, don't let any body that is of the America party to know that I ever sent a letter to you, or that I ever desired you to return my name to the Governour, by no means, if you have any regard to my life; and you will, in keeping it private, greatly oblige me [&c.]

Shubael Lovell, of Barnstable
Living at Hingham

P.S. Pray, sir, be pleased to accept a few vegetables, to be delivered to you by Doctor [Samuel] Gelston, a bold and staunch friend to Government and me.

S. Lovell. (n.2-1143)

November 30, 1775, Philadelphia

Extract from Starbuck, *The History of Nantucket* (1924)

The Continental Congress considered an application that Captain Jenkins be permitted to take a quantity of provisions for the internal consumption of the inhabitants of Nantucket, the reason being that the Committee of Falmouth was unable to supply them and had recommended him to Congress to be supplied with the same at some port in the middle or southern colonies, and ordered that permission be granted the Captain giving bond and taking oath to the committee of inspection of this city, to pursue their instructions in his voyage, and to use his utmost endeavor not to fall into the power of the cutters or armed vessels of the enemy. (s.189)

December 11, 1775, Falmouth

Selectmen and Committees of Falmouth
To the Massachusetts General Court

To the Honble Council and house of Representatives in general Court assembled—

The petition of the select men, and committees of correspondence and inspec'on of the town of Falmouth, in the County of Barnstable, in behalf of the inhabitants of sd Town sheweth—That in the Island called Nashon, one of the Elizabeths Islands is a very commodious harbour, known by the name of Tarpaulin Cove, much used by all vessels passing thro' the Vineyard sound, and where a small ship of war, and two or three tenders being placed might intercept and even destroy all the unarmed vessels passing thro' the sd sound, and all vessels in Buzzards Bay, which will include the  coast from Cape Cod to Rhode Island; and may also from thence be able to make discents upon the coast and take off stock and provisions for the supply of our enemies;—For the preventing of which there has been hitherto a company of men, raised by the wisdom of our government and stationed there which has greatly molested the ministerial ships in harbouring in sd Tarpaulin Cove, and hindered their landing on sd Nashon Island; — And we humbly conceive that if a company of men be continued at sd Cove with a number of canon planted at sd harbour, they would render it a very uncomfortable station for the ministerial ships, and keep them at a proper distance, and deter them from landing and taking off the stock which is very valuable on sd Island, and also be very beneficial to the trade of the country and a great security to us on this exposed sea coast — Likewise that some suitable man in this town may be appointed to muster sd company —

Furthermore your petitioners shew, That in the west end of this sd Town of Falmouth there is a harbour called Woods Hole, very convenient for the Rendezvous of privateers or armed vessels where they will be safe from the attacks of the enemies ships of war. And as they have taken our vessels and employed them in their service, for carrying stock and provisions, to our great grief and mortification, taken forceably from us and our neighbors, and transported it, before our eyes, for the supply of our enemies and oppressors in Boston; —

And in your great wisdom, if you should see fit to allow us two privateers, or armed vessels to defend our sea coasts, and to take their ships and transports, and such of our own vessels, as they have wrested from us — Therefore Hoping the honble court will take these things into your consideration, and provide for the security of this much exposed town & sea coast, as your approved wisdom shall direct; And your petitioners shall ever pray &c —

Committee of Inspection
Jo Palmer
Samuel Fish
Daniel Batles
Selectmen
Tim Crocker
Nathll Shiverick
Committee of Correspondence
Bart Bassett
Job Parker
Nathll Shiverick
Noah Davis (n.3-53)

December 12, 1775, Sandwich

Colonel Nathaniel Freeman to George Washington
Sandwich, December 12, 1775

May it please your Excellency:

Colonel Otis, the younger, the author of the letter to your Excellency enclosed herewith, sent the same open to me, as we were together in ordering Mr. Lovell apprehended and sent a prisoner to your Excellency. Upon reading it, I thought it would not be improper to add, that the two Lovells mentioned in this delinquent's letter, owned that they told Shubael Lovell, the prisoner, they wished he had returned their names to the King's officers as friends to Government, and as having refused to take up arms, &c.

This Shubael, though he appears an ignorant fellow, hath considerable influence among the Barnstable Tories, hath practiced coasting to Nantucket the summer past, and I have no doubt hath communicated every thing of intelligence to the navy, if not frequently supplied them with provisions. Doctor Gelston, to whom he alludes in his letter, we have taken a number of depositions of his having supplied them considerably from Nantucket. He swears he will do it in defiance of the people, and threatens communicating the small-pox to anyone who resists him. I wish he was taken, but cannot get anyone, as yet, to join me in sending on for him. I hope your Excellency will take care that he is taken. The depositions concerning him are now in the hands of Joseph Nye, Esq., at the General Court. I shall be furnished with more, and be at Head-Quarters with Colonel Otis, this week, by Thursday, when shall take the Liberty to wait on your Excellency. In the mean time, I am [&c.]

Nth Freeman. (n.3-65)

Colonel Joseph Otis to George Washington
Barnstable, December 12, 1775

May it please your Excellency:
    The enclosed letter was sent me by the Governour of Rhode Island, on the receipt of which, with the advice of the Field Officers of this regiment, I took up the writer, and, with the advise of Colonel Otis, have sent the man to your Excellency, by Lieutenant Lothrop. The two men mentioned in the letter, we talked with, but have dismissed them till further orders, as there was no proof against them but their being mentioned in the letter sent Captain Ayscough.
    As to Mr. Lovell's character and situation, he is one that we have always looked upon as a Tory, and something busy in the Opposition. He has a large family of small children that want his assistance. I pity the man's folly. As I shall be at Head-Quarters this week, with the Militia ordered from this regiment, shall do myself the honour to wait on you further about the matter. Should be glad Lieut. Lothrop might have the care of him till I see your Excellency. I am [&c.] (n.3-66)

December 18, 1775, Watertown

Executive Records of the Massachusetts Council [Watertown]
Present in Council, Monday December 18, 1775

Read & on the Examination of the said Shubael Lovell by the Major Part of the Council, Ordered that the said Shubael Lovell be sent to the Gaol in Plymouth & there held in close confinement unless he give Bond, with good Security for the Liberty of the Yard, & to be supported there at his own Expence, untill the  further Order of the Major Part of the Council, And that a Mittimus go to the Keeper of the said Gaol accordingly. (n.3-150)

December 18, 1775, Sandwich

Extract from Freeman,
History of Cape Cod, Annals of Barnstable County (1858)

...Nantucket, Martha's Vineyard, and the Elizabeth Isles were positions uncontrollable by patriotic zeal. Depredations from these lurking places of the disaffected and from the enemy were constantly occurring. So vital had become the importance of applying some remedy, that, December 18, after due consideration by the Council and House, special action was had, and Major Joseph Dimmick was commissioned to begin the work of reform. He was directed to embrace an early opportunity and with sufficient aid "repair to Nantucket, and arrest such as are guilty of supplying the enemy with provisions." The disinterested patriotism, the indomitable energy, the unflinching courage of Dimmick of Falmouth have long since passed into a proverb. (f.I-482)

December 28, 1775, Sandwich

Extract from Freeman,
History of Cape Cod, Annals of Barnstable County (1858)

...Col. Freeman of Sandwich was appointed to issue the documents necessary for the "new defence establishment." The officers selected to command the forces at Martha's Vineyard and the Elizabeth Islands, were Barachiah Bassett, major; for company I, Nathan Smith Capt., Jeremiah Manter 1st lt., Fortunatus Bassett, 2d Lt.; for comp. 2, Benj. Smith Capt., Melatiah Davis 1st Lt., James Shaw 2d lt.; for comp. 8, John Grannis Capt., James Blossom 1st Lt., Sam. Hallett 2d Lt.; and for comp. 4, Elisha Nye capt., Steph. Nye Jr. 1st Lt., and John Russell 2d Lt. (f.I-483)

December 30, 1775, Nantucket

Dr. Samuel Gelston (1727-82), Variolator

...In November 1775 a British warship [*Swan*] anchored outside Sherborn [Sherburne, Nantucket] harbor for two weeks and during that period seized, searched, and robbed whatever its captain fancied. Islanders with Loyalist sentiments visited its Captain Ayscough and his wife on shipboard and provided them with bread and other provisions. Dr. [Samuel] Gelston, outspoken in his loyalty to the Crown, was among this group. Reprisal was prompt: on 30 December, Major Joseph Dimmick came from Falmouth with eight provincial soldiers and a warrant for his arrest. He was seized and taken off to the Plymouth jail on suspicion of giving aid and counsel to the enemy. On 22 January 1776, the Massachusetts General Court voted that Samuel Gelston be put under bond for disloyal behavior. Shortly thereafter he escaped to Newport, Rhode Island. A handbill promising a reward for his capture described him as of Nantucket, "a short well set man; had on when he went away a reddish sheepskin coat, dressed with the wool inside, and a scarlet waistcoat." Subsequently apprehended, he was held prisoner at Tarpaulin Cove on Naushon, largest of the Elizabeth Islands, during June 1776.[2]

January 29, 1776, Newport

Brigadier General William West to Governor Nicholas Cooke
Headquarters Febuary the 1: 1776

Sir:
...the Twenty Ninth Instant [sic] a Reved at head qurters an Exspres from warter town with an advertesement from the Jeneral Court for taking up one Docter Gilston of nantucket who has proved him Self Inmical to the Liberties of this Country and was in there Custady who By the assistance of one John Brown

w[h]o once useed to Drive a Coach from providance to Boston made his ascape to new port Said Exspress aplied to me for asistance I Emeately Sent Capt Bartan [William Barton] with a few men insearch of Said Dot gilston and in about one oure had the said Docter and Brown in Custody. Have Sent them Down to the

---

[2] Fred B. Rogers, *Journal of the History of Medicine and Allied Sciences*, Jan. 1972, Vol 27:81-85.

Jeneral Court to Recive there Just Deserts. The Doctor gve Brown thirty Dollers and a good horse paid all Exspe[n]ce to Bring him to new port. The Dor said Brown agreed with him for the money and horse to Carry him where the Devel would not find him. I am [&c.]

Wm West (n.3-1082)

Dr. Samuel Gelston and
"The Speckled Monster of Gravelly Island"
By James Everett Grieder

Into the midst of the controversy over inoculation and the beginnings of yet another [smallpox] epidemic stepped Dr. Samuel Gelston. Born in the village of Southampton on Long Island on March 24th, 1727, Gelston apparently spent the first twenty-five years of his life quite close to home, returning there after receiving his doctorate to take up the life of a country doctor. What eventually prompted him to move away and take up the campaign for inoculation remains unclear, but perhaps it had something to do with what is inscribed on a tombstone in nearby Southold: *In Memory of Elizabeth Wife of Dr. Samuel GELSTON who died 10 Jul 1760 Age 35 yrs, 4 mos.*

No mention is made of the cause of Elizabeth Gelston's death. It may have been smallpox, but then again it may simply be that the recurring pain of remaining in a once-happy place — now marred by grief and premature loss — was too much to bear.

Whatever Dr. Gelston's motivation, his arrival in Massachusetts was well-timed. In 1763 Gelston established a smallpox hospital in Holmes Hole on Martha's Vineyard. The harbor there was bustling with trading vessels from ports all along the Atlantic seaboard and was a natural choice for such a facility. In August of that year, the town gave Dr. Gelston permission to "Cary on and Practice Inoculation of the Small Pox in Soume Suitable Place at Homeses hole," but it was made clear that he was totally on his own. Not only was he required to treat all comers, with no assistance from the town, he also had to pay six shillings for every person inoculated. How these fees were paid is not indicated, but since the arrangement was renewed the following year it must not have been onerous to do so.

Dr. Gelston next turns up on Noddle's Island in Boston Harbor during the 1764 smallpox outbreak. According to Samuel Drake's *History of Boston*, "...when the smallpox raged in Boston, the physicians removed their inoculating hospital from Castle William [present-day Castle Island in Dorchester near the JFK Library] to Noddle's Island, at the mansion-house where Robert Temple, Esq. had lately resided, "which contained elegant rooms, suitable for the reception of persons of the first condition. One of the physicians, Dr. Gelston, to remain constantly on the island, and the others were to attend when desired." Prior to the establishment of the hospitals at Castle William and on Noddle's Island smallpox victims were left on the shore of nearby Spectacle Island to meet their ghastly fate all alone.

Apparently Dr. Gelston never stayed in one place for long (or was never allowed to do so) because he next surfaces in Nantucket in 1769, again looking for a place to establish another smallpox hospital. Nantucket had been flirting with establishing some kind of facility for some time; Edouard Stackpole notes in his monograph "Dr. Samuel Gelston—Medical Pioneer" (*Historic Nantucket*, Vol. 31, No. 3, 1984):

> ...there had been efforts to establish houses where inoculation could be practiced, the first area being on Coatue Point in October, 1763. But this vote of the Town was rescinded the following month, and a new area designated, this being at Shimmo.

The following summer the town voted to reconsider the vote of the previous year, and banned the practice of inoculation altogether. Clearly, the residents of the island had mixed feelings about the whole thing.

When Dr. Gelston arrived on the island, the initial hostility to his plan melted swiftly in the face of the good doctor's enthusiasm and charisma. He managed to convince the selectmen of the Town that he could safely establish a smallpox hospital in a remote location, and set about finding one. The place Gelston chose was little more than a pebble-strewn hump that rose a few feet about the pounding surf, and was called Gravelly Island by the locals (located between Tuckernuck and Muskeget, Gravelly Island endured until the late nineteenth century before succumbing to the sea's relentless pull). Accordingly, Dr. Gelston arranged for the construction of a sturdy little building and began inoculating patients as soon as it was completed.

The harmony between the doctor and the Town did not last long. Apparently some of the patients of Gravelly Island decided that they did not want to spend the mandatory three weeks of recuperatory time on their little shoal of respite, and left early. The local townsfolk, understandably alarmed at the thought of smallpox-infected visitors roaming Nantucket at will, shifted once again in their opinion of the whole affair and sought to shut down the hospital—the problem was that there was no legal way to do it. Apparently Gravelly Island, along with Muskeget, lay outside of the jurisdiction of Nantucket; "apparently" because the Town had to resort to a petition originating from a June 6, 1771 Town Meeting, at which it was voted that Abishai Folger, Esq., Zaccheus Macy, Frederick Folger, Josiah Barker, and Timothy Folger draw up and forward said petition to the General Court in Boston asking that the two islands be annexed to Nantucket.

At yet another Town Meeting held in September of that year it was voted "...that a remonstrance be sent to the Governor to lay the state of inoculation before him in a true light, and to desire him to sign a bill to annex Musketet and Gravelly Islands to this County...." Meanwhile the wheels of government continued to grind slowly along: a bill passed both branches of the Legislature approving the annexation, but the governor refused to sign it, leaving the Town without legal recourse.

Their last hope in Boston fading away, the Town decided to simply offer to buy out Dr. Gelston's investment in the hospital, lock, stock, and variolation needle, and appropriated the money at a June 1772 Town Meeting. The letter from Dr. Gelston laying out the terms of purchase still exists, and is on record at the Town Clerk's office. Written in Dr. Gelston's firm, clear hand, he notes that "as this Town seems amicably disposed to put an end to the Long prevailing controversy, Respecting my inoculating at Gravel Island" the good doctor was willing to consider terms but felt that "...such a compensation (at least) aught to be made me as will be adequate to the Real & Intrinsic cost of my Buildings." The page following his letter totals up all of his expenses (including grog for the workmen) and arrives at a figure of £1072 and change, which is roughly $175,000 in 2005 dollars (a bargain by Nantucket standards). The bill was paid, and Dr. Gelston ceased his inoculations.

This is not quite the end of the story, however. Dr. Gelston had built up quite a reputation as a general physician on Nantucket (in spite of his mad scientist leanings), and decided to settle here. When the Revolution broke out a few years later, Dr. Gelston stood out as a vociferous Tory on a island known to be rather less than enthusiastic about the Continental cause; in fact, Gelston's views were so well known that his arrest was ordered by the mainland authorities, and men were dispatched to haul him off to the jail in Plymouth. Gelston escaped from confinement with outside help and returned to the island; the following notice appeared in local newspapers:

ADVERTISEMENT.

Watertown, January 26, 1776.

RAN AWAY from the custody of the Messenger of the General Court, a certain Dr. Samuel Gelston, belonging to Nantucket, a short well set man; had on when he went away a reddish Sheepskin coat, dress'd with the wool inside, and a scarlet waistcoat; he was apprehended as an enemy to this country, 'tis suppos'd he will attempt escaping to the enemy, by the way of Nantucket, Rhode-Island, or New-York.------Whoever will take up said Gelston and deliver him to the messenger of the House of Representatives, shall be well rewarded for his time and expence.

William Story, Nathaniel Freeman, Ebenezer White, } Committee of the House of Representatives

Notice for the Arrest of Dr. Samuel Gelston.

ADVERTISEMENT.

Watertown. January 26, 1776.

Ran away from the custody of the messenger of the General Court, a certain *Dr. Samuel Gelston*, belonging to *Nantucket*; a short well fed man; had on when he went away a reddish Sheepskin coat, dress'd with the wool inside, and a scarlet waistcoat; he was apprehended as an enemy to this country, 'tis suppos'd he will attempt escaping to the enemy, by the way of Nantucket, Rhode-Island, or New York. ----- Whoever will take up said Gelston and deliver him to the messenger of the House of representatives, shall be well rewarded for his time and expence.

[Signed]

William Story,	Committee of
Nathaniel Freeman,	the House of
Ebenezer White,	representatives

Gelston was recaptured and jailed again. This time he and his supporters resorted to petitioning the Legislature for his release, a request that was eventually granted. Dr. Gelston returned home to Nantucket and continued to serve the island, primarily as a doctor but also, on one notable occasion, as a negotiator: a fleet of Tory privateers was threatening to raid Nantucket for supplies, and Gelston managed to persuade them to spare the island, presumably using some of that old charisma of his. Dr. Gelston died on July 6, 1782 at the age of only fifty-eight. Although he and his son Roland were long-remembered as respected physicians on Nantucket, it is in his role as scientific pioneer that Dr. Gelston's true gift to humanity lay. In the end, he was brought to earth by those who feared that the good doctor's attempts to tame the Speckled Monster [smallpox] would instead release its fury upon the people of Nantucket.[3]

---

[3] http://tuckernuckjim.tripod.com/hidden/id14.html

Smart Scurmey.

5

The Vineyard Seacoast Company

March 6, 1776, Edgartown

Beriah Norton to James Otis
Edgartown, March 9th 1776, to Be Com[m]unicated to
The Honol James Otis Esqr President of the Honol Council
At Watertown

These are to in form your honr that about five o'Clock In the morning of the Sixth of march Instant the Sloop *francis* william furnell Prisemaster was Shipracked on the South Side of the Island of Marthers Vinyard. Sd Sloop was taken By the Ship *Phenex* of the British Navy about the 13th of December Last as Sd Prisemaster Sath, and was the Property of william Lowther Esqr Merchant in New York & Bound for Boston

By the way of Newport, the Salors Being taken in to Custody and also the Vessel and Cargo the Captors forthwith made Information to me I went to the Rack and appointed major Doggett to take An Invent[o]ry of her Cargo which is as followeth about 50 hog[sheads] tobaco 190 Barrels terpentine 3 M & ½ Staves 24 half hides &C and the men ordered under gard of the Sea Co[a]st Men.

The Next morning there Was Information in town that there was a transport Ship at Anchor, Near Nantucket Sholes. I Not Being in town my Self till the afternoon when I found there was about 37 men gone of[f] to Ingage the Ship, with a Small Sloop, about 23 of our men ware those of the Sea Co[a]st under Capt Benjn Smith the [rest] ware of the militia thay Ingaged hur and after a Smart Scurmey the Capt of the Ship Being Shot thru the [torn] thie Struck to our Yanke Sloop and are Brought in the old town harbour.

The Capt is in a fare way of recovery. hur Cargo is about 100 Charldren of Colt 100 Butts of Porter, 30 hoge Sower Crout Puttators and Sundry outher Artacils, the officers and Sea men are ordered to had Quorters By the Sea Coast. Capt under the Care of Second Lieutenant James Shaw. I shall Not Inlarg Any farther on the Subject as I Expect to Be at Court within 15 Days. I would Jest Remind your honor that the Resolve for Removeing the restraint of our trade hath Not Been Published to My Knowledge, And as we have Sufered By it alredy I Must humbly Beg your honor to have it Published as Soon as Posable Several Persons haveing Been abliged to unlode there Vessels Alredy that was Bound here On that Acct I have only to Say that the two Gentlemen the Prise Master above said and Mr James Christie Passeng[e]r on Bord the Ship have Beh'aved them Selves with honor while in this Town— from your honos [&c.]

[Col] Beriah Norton

N.B. these Certifie your honor that Capt Richerd Wellen a worthy gentleman Lately appointed Capt of the first Company of Militia in this Regiment had the Command in takeing the Ship as Master—Benjn Smith within Named As Capt But I Expect to Be Down Soon. Yours [&c.]

[Col.] Beriah Norton (n.4-257)

March 7, 1776, Edgartown

Captain Benjamin Smith to the Massachusetts Council
Edgartown, March 10, 1776

Gentlemen, I have only Time to Inform your honours That on the 7th Inst I with A Detachment of my Compny with Some Gentlemen of This Town, in number All About fourty, with A small vessel engaged for the purpose; Engaged And Tooke The Ship *Harriot* Weymse Orrock master Store Ship from London bound for Boston, Laden with Cole Porter and Potatos; 2 And have sent The mate (The Capt being wounded in the Engagement) with fourteen Mariners by Leut [James] Shaw And have Directed him To Deliver Them To The Honourbl Council, I Am Endeavring To secure The property by Giting the Ship To the mane, which having Perfected, Shall give Immediate Attendance for farther Direction in the matter; And in The Interim Remain your Honrs [&c.]

Benjamin Smith (n.4-281)

Letter of the Mate of the *Harriot*
London Chronicle, June 27 to June 29, 1776

By a letter from the Mate of the *Harriot*, Capt. Orrock, a transport, which left the Downs the 10th of December, with stores, provisions, &c. for our troops at Boston, there is advice, that after greatly suffering on their passage by storms, they at length got to the Jerseys, and after being refitted by the assistance of the carpenters of his Majesty's ship the *Phoenix*, Capt. Parker ordered them to proceed for Rhode Island, in hopes they might there meet a convoy to see them through the Nantucket shoals:

They left New York March 4, at night, and after three days terrible weather the ship grounded among shoals; at length the gale abating, the long-boat was hoisted out, and manned with the boatswain and four seamen, to go to the nearest land for a pilot and assistance.

The 7th of March (says the writer) we saw a sloop making towards us; she run under our stern full of men; they asked if we wanted a pilot; the Captain said he did, and requested one to be sent: They sent a boat with four men, and one was left in the

Harriot as a pilot, who asked the Captain how many hands he had? It was answered, that five men were sent on shore, and that only two were left. The pretended Pilot then offered to send for two or three out of the sloop, but he called after the boat, to send all the men the boat could carry; on which Capt. Orrock began to suspect something, and asked the Pilot whether he intended to take the ship? To which no satisfactory answer was given; the arms were then ordered upon deck; which consisted of six very indifferent muskets, six old cutlasses, with two swivel guns on the ship's bows. The Captain ordered the Pilot to carry the ship through the shoals, else he would put him to instant death; but the man begged for mercy, declared he was ignorant of the place, and incapable of doing it; and was ordered to the cabbin.

About this time we saw our boat making for us from the shore; but the sloops people seeing her also, bore down and took the boat, and in a few minutes the ship [sic sloop] bore down upon us, within musket shot, with about fifty men in her; they fired a volley of small arms at us; we returned a fire from our swivels and small arms, and continued the engagement for half an hour; being in want of shot, having only nine balls at first for the swivels, we took the lead from the Cook's hearth, and cut it into slugs, resolved not to surrender while we had ammunition left; at last Capt. Orrock, whose intrepidity and courage cannot be too much commended, took one of the swivels in his arms, to carry it aft the ship, and whilst in the act of pointing it and firing, was shot through the fleshy part of his thigh; he fell on the deck, and was carried to his cabin, bleeding very much.

This misfortune deprived us of one of our bravest hands, our ammunition also spent, the ship aground, and no hopes of escape now remained; I, therefore, by the Captain's consent, gave the ship up to the Americans, who took possession of her. They were such dastards, that they placed our five men, whom they had taken in the boat, before some of them, and rested their muskets on the men's shoulders, to screen themselves from our shot: They were a set of ruffians, and a disgrace to the name of men; by experience we found them far short in true courage to Englishmen; for fifty of them well armed, and supplied with powder and ball, their sloop afloat, and our ship on shore, did not dare to board us, which they might have done, as the sloop drew little water. As soon as they came on board, they eat and drank the Captain's provisions and liquors, set butts of porter on end, and stove in their heads, to drink greedily, rummaged and plundered every thing, taking even our clothes from us. The only instance of humanity they shewed, was, they sent Captain Orrock ashore with some degree of tenderness to the pretended pilot's house, put him to bed, and got a surgeon to dress his wound, and before I left America I had the pleasure to hear he was getting well. We were carried to an island named Martha's Vineyard, a mile and a half from the main land of New England, from thence Mr. Christie, an officer of the army, who was a passenger with us from New York, and all our crew, were conveyed in the sloop which took us to Plymouth, where we were examined by a committee of the town, and then sent, under a strong guard, to the head quarters at Cambridge, where we were put into a prison; but by the favour of Gen. Washington I was released the same day; also my brother, a boy. (n.4-281)

March 17, 1776, Boston

Memoirs of Major General William Heath
[Cambridge] 17th [March]

In the morning the British evacuated Boston; their rear guard with some marks of precipitation. A number of cannon were left spiked and two large marine mortars, which they in vain attempted to burst.... The troops on the Roxbury side, moved over the Neck and took possession of Boston; as did others from Cambridge, in boats. On the Americans entering the town, the inhabitants discovered joy inexpressible. The town had been much injured in its buildings, and some individuals had been plundered. Some British stores were left. The British army went on board their transports below the Castle. A number of American adherents to them, and the British cause, went away with the army. (n.4-378)

April 7, 1776, Holmes Hole

Boston Gazette, **Monday, April 22, 1776**
Watertown, April 22d.

The Schooner [*Violenti*] capt. [Stephen] Cleveland, which sailed from Salem for Winyaw, in North Carolina, the beginning of

January last, was taken on her passage by the *Scarborough* man of war, and sent to Georgia, where after lading with rum, sugar, &c. She proceeded for Boston, when on last Friday 7 night (not knowing the ministerial fleet and army had evacuated that place) meeting with a heavy gale of wind, she put into the Vineyard, where she was properly taken care of by some boats from thence. — One Marsh, the master's mate, and a son of commodore Loring, as master's mate, with two passengers on board, were bro't to town for examination on Saturday last. (n.4-1191)

April 16, 1776, Martha's Vineyard

Major Barachiah Bassett to the
Commander of the Continental Forces at Boston

Sir

I have sent you under the Care of a Sergeant four prisoners taken aboard the Schooner *Valenti* at Martha's Vineyard bound for Boston — Viz: Edward Marsh, Master the Mate, & two passengers in the employment of the Ministerial Forces I am Sir [&c.]

Bar^h Bassett Majr in the Provincial Forces (n.4-846)

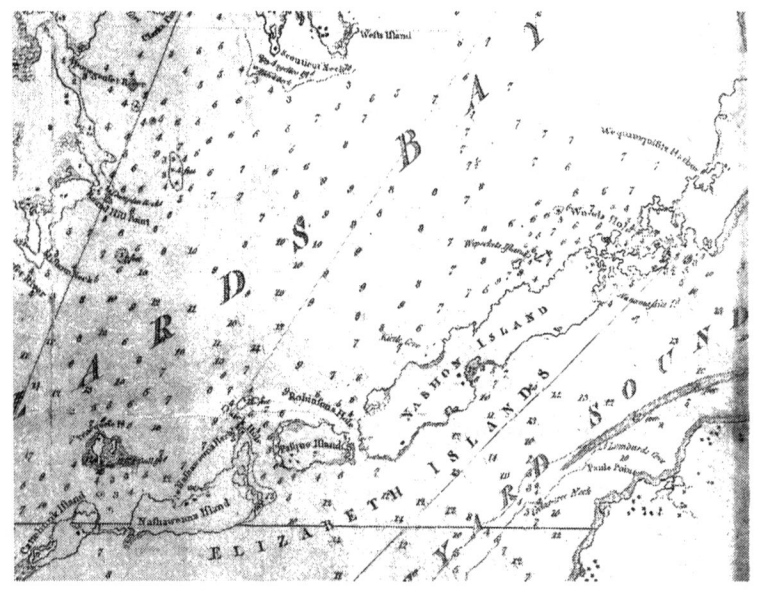

The Elizabeth Islands. Des Barres, 1776.

6

Defense of the Elizabeth Islands

June 11, 1776, Tarpaulin Cove

Barachiah Bassett to the Massachusetts General Court

To the Honle the Council and the Honl House of Representatives of the Massachusets Bay

    In pursuance to a Resolve of the Court, have Removed the Four pieces of cannon from Trurro to the Eliz[abet]h Islands. I Am Bound in Duty to let you know there is no Use for them without Ball, Ladles &c. which Renders them fitt for use—Whereas, if they were Supply'd with those Materials, they would be of uncommon advantage toward protecting the posts they are Design'd for,— should your Honrs Consider the Situation & Advantage of the posts, I doubt not but you would allow said Materials as also

Intrenching Tools which must be used for the protection of said posts—

Permit me also to Acquaint your Honrs that it is not in my power to afford the protection which is Necessary to the Islands Westward of Tarpolan Cove Island, & the Vessels that are Continualy passing without I have at least Ten Whale Boats— Therefore pray that some Measure may be taken for the provison of the Foregoing—Gentlemen your most Devoted [&c.]

Barachiah Bassett (n.5-471)

June 18, 1776, Tarpaulin Cove

Major Barachiah Bassett to the Massachusetts Council

Hon. Council of the Massachusetts Bay

In pursuant of your Orders I have sent Capt John Grannis and brought Dr. Saml. Gilson [Gelston] to the Elizabeth Island, where he is under the care of my Party.

As to the Schooner said Gilson came In [*Peggy*]; I have Taken Her and sent her to Dartmouth and put her under the care of Capt. Hilyard Mayhew until further Orders from your Honors. Have sent you the Expences by Capt. Grannis. Gentlemen [&c.]

Barachiah Bassett (n.5-298)

June 22, 1776, Watertown

Acts and Resolves of the Massachusetts General Court

Whereas the four Cannon mentioned in said Return made to this Court by Major Basset, are proper for Sea Service, and the Armed Brig belonging to this Colony at Dartmouth is in want of the same, and with them can procede on a cruize—therefore—

Resolved, That Thomas Durfee Esqr one of the Committee for fitting out the said Brig, be, and he hereby is empowered, & directed to cause the said Cannon forthwith to be Removed, and put on board said Brig and the said Committee are also directed to get the said Brig in readiness for a Cruize as soon as may be. Also,

Resolved that in lieu of the said four Cannon, there be placed at Tarpaulin Cove Harbor, two pieces of Cannon—nine pounders, and the Commissary General is hereby directed to deliver the same to Mr Durfee on his order, to be conveyed to Major Basset, and also to deliver 100 nine shot together with ladels, and the necessary apparatus for the said two Cannon, And that the said Basset cause the same to be fited, & mounted as soon as may be for the Defence of said Harbor: — and it is also

Resolved, that the hon: Walter Spooner Esqr be, and hereby is directed, & empowered to provide ten old Whale Boats that are fit to be protection of the neighbouring Islands, and the Shipping coming in, and going out, and also purchase twelve Shovels, six Spades, and four pick axes — the same to be for the use of said Basset, and Men under his Command in the Service aforesaid and the said Walter Spooner is directed to lay his Accompt before this Court for payment thereof

Resolved That the Commissary General be, and he is hereby directed to deliver to Thomas Durfee Esqr out of the Colony Stores now at Dartmouth in the care of Mr Lemuel Williams, four Cannon, four pounders, fourteen Swivel Guns, twelve blunderbusses, Eighty Cutlasses two thousand pound weight of Gunpowder, One Tun, & a half of four pound Shot, Six hundred swivel Gun Shott, Seventy Hand grenadoes, Sixty Small Arms, seven hundred pound of Sheet Lead for the use of the Brigg called the *Rising Empire*. (n.5-676)

July 3, 1776, Philadelphia

John Adams to Abigail Adams

Your Favour of June 17, dated at Plymouth, was handed me, by Yesterdays Post. I was much pleased to find that you had taken a Journey to Plymouth, to see your Friends in the long Absence of one whom you may wish to see. The Excursion will be an Amusement, and will serve your Health. How happy would it have made me to have taken this Journey with you?

I was informed, a day or two before the Receipt of your Letter, that you was gone to Plymouth, by Mrs. Polly Palmer, who was obliging enough in your Absence, to inform me of the Particulars of the Expedition to the lower Harbour against the Men of War. Her Narration is executed, with a Precision and Perspicuity which would have become the Pen of an accomplished Historian.

I am very glad you had so good an opportunity of seeing one of our little American Men of War [brig *Defence*]. Many Ideas, new to you, must have presented themselves in such a Scene; and you will in future, better understand the Relations of Sea Engagements....

Yesterday the greatest Question was decided which ever was debated in America, and a greater perhaps, never was or will be decided among Men. A Resolution was passed without dissenting Colony "that these united Colonies, are, and of right ought to be free and independent States, and as such, they have, and of Right ought to have full Power to make War, conclude Peace, establish Commerce, and to do all the other Acts and Things, which other States may rightfully do." You will see in a few days a Declaration setting forth the Causes, which have impell'd Us to this mighty Revolution, and the Reasons which will justify it, in the Sight of God and Man. A Plan of Confederation will be taken up in a few days.... (n.5-898)

November 1776, Holmes Hole

Excerpt from *Martha's Vineyard*, by Henry Franklin Norton

During the Revolution this harbor was the refuge for many British men-of-war. In 1775 the people of Homes Hole erected a "liberty pole" on Manter's Hill. As another expression of public feeling the women threw all their tea into the hole to show their attitude regarding the Boston Port Bill. A few months later the British ship *Unicorn* came into the harbor looking for a pole to replace a spar lost in a storm. The captain spying this "liberty pole" sent word to the selectmen that he would purchase "the pole on the hill"; and if they refused to sell it, he would consider it a rebellious act and fire on the town. The selectmen set a price, not daring to do otherwise, and the captain informed them that his men would take the pole the next day.

Mr. Daggett, one of the selectmen, upon reaching home related this incident. His daughter Polly made no comment, but as soon as supper was over she went to Parnel Manter, a friend and told her the story. These girls made up their minds that the British could not have the "liberty pole." While the girls were trying to think of some way to save the pole from the British, Maria Allen came in. As the three girls were discussing a plan, suddenly one of them said: "I have an idea, let's blow up the pole."

How this could be done was a great problem to the girls. Maria Allen said that there was a ship's auger in her father's shop; they could bore a hole in the pole and fill it with powder. Parnel Manter could borrow her father's powder-horn. Maria secured the auger, Parnel the powder-horn. Then the three girls started for Manter's Hill. They arrived at the pole and started to bore, each taking her turn. Two holes were made and filled to the brim with powder, Polly Daggett giving the hem of her woolen petticoat for wads. Everything now being in readiness, the question was how to ignite the powder. At last Polly solved the problem. She would get a beanpole from a neighboring field, tie the rest of her petticoat hem on it, set it on fire, and push it against the powder. Polly ran home and stole a warming-pan full of hot coals from the fireplace. The critical moment had arrived. Who would dare to touch it off? They lighted the cloth on the end of the bean-pole and all three shoved it against the woolen wads. After the third attempt the wads started to burn; then the girls dropped the bean-pole and ran for shelter behind an old barn. A second later there came a report like that of a cannon; then the splitting and crackling of the pole. The next instant came a second explosion which completely destroyed the pole, making it useless. The girls then hurried home, not mentioning the incident until many years after the war.

The next morning the captain of the *Unicorn* sent men ashore to get the pole. When they saw the condition it was in they were furious and reported to their commander. The captain went to the selectmen only to learn that they were as puzzled as anyone about the affair. The *Unicorn* was finally obliged to sail away without obtaining the desired spar.[4]

December 7, 1776, Naushon Island

Boston Gazette, **Monday, December 16, 1776**

The Enemy are in Possession of Newport, in Rhode-Island, but what Number we have not learnt; and we hear that the noted

---

[4] Henry Franklin Norton, *Martha's Vineyard*, published by Henry Franklin Norton and Robert Emmett Pyne, 1923, pp. 57-68.

Joseph Wanton, Esq; is appointed Governor of the same, and has given Orders for those who desire Protection from (what is called) Government, to affix a White Flag to their respective Houses.

We learn, That on Friday last four Vessels, belonging to the Enemy landed about 200 Troops on the Elizabeth Islands, and Plundered from thence about 200 Sheep, besides burning a House and Barn, belonging to Mr. John Read of this Town.... (n.7-493)

**Captain John Macartney, R. N., to
Commodore Sir Peter Parker,** *Ambuscade*
in Rhode Island Harbour, 12th December 1776

Sir: Captain Feilding [Charles Fielding] onboard His Majesty's Frigate the *Diamond*, with His Majesty's Frigate the *Ambuscade* under my Command, being at Anchor in Martha's Vineyard Sound, lying there to intercept the Rebel Privateers from getting out from Rhode Island; On Saturday 7th Instant Captain Fielding, the Senior Officer, sent his Barge onshore to Nashawn Island with a Flag of Truce, intending to purchase fresh Stock for his people; but to our very great Surprize about 10 or 12 of the Rebels, against the Laws of God and Man, fired at the Boat, and shot the gunner through the Head, but did not kill him.

Captain Fielding very justly enraged at this, ordered me to send all the Boats manned and armed, with the whole party of Marines, which was immediately complied with, under the Command of Lieut. Patrick Sinclair, 2d Lieutenant of the Ship, Lieutenants Anderson and Gregg of the Marines, who all repaired onboard the *Diamond* which weighed and stood close in-Shore; and after firing some of her great Guns to scour the Beach, sent her own and *Ambuscade's* Men onshore to the Number of between 130 and 140; who after making their Landing good amidst a very galling, straggling Firing from behind Rocks, Walls &ca. Drove all the Rebels, now grown pretty numerous, from off the Island into some small Vessels on the other Side with the loss of 4 or 5 of their Men killed.

Their villainous Conduct in firing at a Flag of Truce entitled them now to all the Horrors of Rebellion, which was immediately put into Execution, by setting Fire to every thing that would burn; so that neither House, Barn, Hay nor Indian Corn that could be met with escaped the Flames, nor did the live-Stock share a better Fate: for what could not be carried off was shot. All this was done in a few Hours, with only the Loss of one Marine killed belonging to the *Diamond* and two Marines slightly wounded belonging to the *Ambuscade*.

Our Success, Sir, will shew the Conduct and Courage of the Officers and Men upon such occasions; and I flatter myself that this Affair, Sir, will meet with your Approbation, which will always give great pleasure to, Sir [&c.]

John Macartney.

NB. I parted from the *Diamond*, Captain Fielding on Monday the 9th Instant in a very hard Gale of Wind from the NW off Gay Head; She not being able to weather it, stood towards the Sea under her Courses (n.7-456)

Boston Gazette, Monday, December 23, 1776

By a gentleman from Falmouth, we have collected a more particular account of what happened at the Elizabeth islands, on or about the 6th day of December the enemy made their appearance with two ships in the mouth of the Sound between Gay Head and the western most islands, after cruizing two days some of the crew went ashore on the outermost island, where was a little hutt, after buying a few turkeys, asking the price of sheep, and what force was at Tarpaulin Cove, on Naushon Island, they went on board ship again, came to sail and run into Robinson's hole, near which place lived Mr. Jeremiah Robinson, a Quaker, who made not the least opposition to their landing, but his family through fear, which consisted of his wife, an aged mother of 80 years, with 9 or 10 children, fled to the woods for safety.

The enemy landed about 150 men, plundered and burnt the house in which was all the poor man's beef, pork, roots, butter, cheese, &c. together with all his furniture, not content with all this, they burnt his corn barn, in which was all his grain, killed and carried off two or three cattle and hogs, likewise killed and left dead on the ground some of his milch cows, and wounded and mangled others in the most cruel manner—Thus was a peaceable and good liver in a few hours reduced to the greatest distress, by worse than brutal enemies.

Capt. [Benjamin] Nye who was stationed at the Cove, with the help of the militia from the neighbouring towns very soon made a strong party, went up to the west end of the island, but they had gone on board the ships, and the next day stood out of the sound. We have not been able to learn who commanded the ships.

By a Vessel arriv'd at Cape-Ann from Guadaloupe in 19 Days, we learn, that before she sail'd six French men of war and some transports arriv'd there from France, who were part of a fleet that bro't 15,000 troops; and that the Captains of the men of war said they did not doubt but that war was declar'd in France against England before their arrival. (n.7-567)

Attack on Newport, 1778.

**Vice Admiral Richard Lord Howe to
Commodore Sir Peter Parker,** *Eagle*
Off New York, Decr the 22d 1776

....It is with much concern that I have been advised from the Contents of Captain Macartney's Letter of the necessity Captain Fielding deemed himself under to resent the Insult offered to the Flag of Truce he sent to Nashawn Island, in the manner therein stated. If the Inhabitants were conscious of the Deference paid by all civilized Nations to an Intercourse proffered under the Sanction of a Flag of Truce, they certainly merited the severest Treatment. But as I rather suppose they are of a Class wholly uninformed in such Distinctions, I much wish that other expedients had been taken to apprize them of their Misconduct; and that Extremities, which could have no immediate advantage to the King's Service attending them, had been at least postponed.

Nevertheless as things are now circumstanced it becomes necessary that the motives for proceeding to such severities, should be made generally known, Lest an impression should be taken of the King's intentions with regard to the ignorant and misguided part of his disaffected Subjects, different from His Majesty's most gracious purpose in such respects.

You are therefore requested to use every reasonable means, for making those motives, so generally known. And if the Circulation thereof cannot be advanced through the Channel of any intercourse which the Inhabitants of Block Island may probably hold with those of the Elizabeth Islands, and of the adjacent Coasts of the Continent, it is my earnest desire that it may be made an Object of particular Attention, and every requisite facility given to promote it.

And for the same beneficial purposes, You are at liberty, in respect of these Instructions, to grant, and it is advisable to take all suitable Opportunities to allow, the Inhabitants dwelling upon the Coasts adjacent to the Stations of the Ships under your command, the use of their ordinary Fishing-Craft or other means of providing for their daily Subsistence and Support; where the same does not seem liable to any material abuse. And in your Signification thereof to the several Captains, I must desire You will also recommend to them, to encourage and cultivate all amicable correspondence with the said Inhabitants, to gain their good Will and Confidence, whilst they demean themselves in a peaceable and orderly manner. And to grant them every other Indulgence which the Limitations upon their Trade specified in the Act passed the last Session of Parliament for restraining the Commerce of the rebellious Colonies therein mentioned, will consistently admit: In order to conciliate their friendly Dispositions and to detach them from the Prejudices they have imbibed to the Subversion of all legal Authority in the different Provinces concerned.

Having made, from the number of Frigates under your Orders, the dispositions requisite for blocking up the Ports of New London, Westward; Those in Buzzards Bay, Eastward; And the Channels from Providence and the adjacent parts communicating with your present Station; No means offering for getting possession of, or destroying the Armed Vessels of the Enemy, collected in those Retreats, It will be next incumbent to provide similar Restrictions on the New England Ports. In these several instances, I conceive it will be expedient to suggest proper places of Anchorage for the cruising Ships to retire to at times, for enabling them to keep at, or near their Stations, during the ensuing Winter Season. (n.7-554)

December 15, 1776, Boston

Council Chamber to Capt. Elisha Nye
Boston December 17, 1776

Sir;

You are hereby empowered and directed immediately to enlist a company of Men to consist of Sixty eight Men Officers included on the Seacoast Establishment for the defense of the Elizabeth Islands as soon as possible which Company of men when enlisted are to be stationed at Naushon and to obey you as their Captain.

On motion ordered that Thomas Jones be appointed Commissary for supplying with provisions & necessaries the two companys to be raised and stationed on the Elizabeth Islands, as also any militia that shall be called in on an alarm for the defense of said Islands. (e.276)

December 17, 1776, Falmouth

Joseph Dimuck to the Honorable the Council of the State of the Massachusetts Bay

Gentlemen-
You may remember that you gave orders for raising Two Companys To be Stationed on Nashone. The Capts. have Both Ben with me [some time] and say they cannot enlist any men By Reason of the Wages Being so Low. I have Been endeavoring to forward the mater But find that to be the universal Complaint...if your Honors are so pleased to give any further orders about the Mater I shall endeavor to Conduct...Agreable their to.
I am yours to Serve

Joseph Dimuck (e.276)

January 1, 1777, Boston

State of Massachusetts Bay in the House of Representatives

Resolved that the Militia officers of the Town of Falmouth in the Co. of Barnstable be and are hereby directed to detach from the Several Companys in that Town twenty-five able bodied men including one Lieut. two Sergents and two Corporals which officers shall be appointed by the above military officers out of those same ranks in the...Companys. Which men so raised shall be...stationed at the Island of Nawshawn for the Defence of the Harbour of Tarpolin Cove there to remain for...two months unless sooner releived.... To be upon the same establishment and receive the same pay as the four Independant Companies now stationed at Hull near Boston, and it is further resolved that the resolve of this Court of the eleventh Day of December last & the order of Council of 15th. Day of December last for raising Companys for the Defense of said Island be and hereby is repealed and that the order be recalled.
Sent up for Concurrence

Sam. Freeman, Speaker (n.4-281)

Shaving Mills in Action.

7
The Loss of the Elizabeth Islands

January 12, 1778, Falmouth
Elisha Nye to Council of the State of the Massachusetts Bay

Dear Sir;
    I would inform you by what means the ammunition got damaged in bringing it from the Island. I sea it all put in the Boat in good order and put it in the care of Lieutenant Silas Hatch and one of the Sargents to bring of which I thought would take the same Care as if I Had Ben there my Self. But the Boat Sprang a Leak and By their Carlessness they Let the powder stand in the water and got it wet. The Excuse they made when they Had got to woods hole was they Had nothing to Bale water with which was not so, for they had pots and kettles and men enough in the Boats to Keep her free from water if they would. I took all the pains I could to get it off in good order. But the misfortune is happened and must Leve you to Jugg where the Blame Lyes. Likewise I

would inform you one of the boxes of Common Cartridges that was sent up Last Spring [?] have rec'd. which Lyes in Commissary Nickersons [?]
   I am your most obt. Serv.
                                               Elisha Nye (e.279)

January 14, 1778, Penikese Island

Master's Journal of HM Sloop *Haerlem*, Lieutenant John Knight

at 3 AM weigh'd and Came to Sail Stood to the Westward at 4 wind Came ahead bore away and at 5 Came to ag^n. in Pennekees Harbour bearings as before at 8 weigh'd and Came to Sail Stood to the E^{t}ward at 9 Run thro Quickss Hole into the Vineyard Sound and Stood to the Eastwd. Saw a  Schooner Boat Gave Chace fired 4 four Pounders Shotted with round and Grape 2 Swivels and 30 Rounds of small arms to bring To too but she run on shore at Noon...working into Homles's Hole TKd. occasionally

   First and middle Parts Fresh Gales and Cloudy...Latter Fresh Breezes PM at 1 Came too in Homles' Hole in 4 fm^s, veer'd to 1/3 of a Cable the WL Chop NbW EL Chopp NbE. Saw a Sloop Schooner and 2 Pilots Boats at the Head of the Hole, sent a Boat and Br^t them out and anch^d. them Near us. The Boat was fired at from the Shore fired 4 four Pounders Shotted to Cover the Boat. (n.11-117)

January 15, 1778, Holmes Hole

Master's Journal of HM Sloop *Haerlem*, Lieutenant John Knight
Janry 1778 Thursday 15 anchored in Vineyard Haven Harbor

AM Came onb^d. a Flagg of Truce at 3 AM anch^d. by us a Sloop from Connecticut bound to Nantucket with Provisions. Took the Master and hands out sent 5 men to take Charge of her.

Fresh Breezes and Clear weather PM at 1 weigh^d. and Came to Sail Prize Sloop and 2 Pilots Boats in Company Empd. working to the W^t w^d · in the Vineyard Sound TKd. Occasionally, at 4 Came too in Tarpaulin Cove in 3 1/2 fms. water Veer'd to 1/3, of a Cable the W^t. Point of the Cove SW the E^t. Point ENE & a fort at the Head of the Cove N°. (n.11-133)

February 18, 1778, Nantucket Sound

Journal of Marine Captain John Trevett, Ship *Mary* Nantucket and Martha's Vineyard, 18-21 February 1778

…We Saw a Number of Sailes on our Pasage but never Spoke with Any the first Land we Made was the Vinyard! We are now Runing Down for Nantucket itt is now 18 Days Since we Parted with the Sloop *Providence* and we have had Very Cold Wither and hard Gailes out of thirty Men thare is not more then ten but Who has thare Hands & feet froze one Man froze to Death his Name was James Dark. He informed Me When I took him att New Providence that he had bene taken by a British Privatear and that He belonged to Vergenea.

This Day [18 Feb.] we Ankerd under Nantucket the Wind Still blowing Very heard So that we Can not Gett on Shore we firing Signul Guns.

The Next Day [19 Feb.] the Wind Continues Blowing So no boat Can Come on Board I thort itt Nesesere to bure James Dark and we Did itt in a Decent Maner.

The third Day [20 Feb.] Several Bots from Shore Came on Board being Very Short of Provison Sent on Shore and Purchesed fife [five] Sheep So we ware well Provided with Fresh Pork; 3 the Wind Abates now A Sail in Sight Runing Down the South Side of Nantucket [HMS *Haerlem*]; the Nantucket Men not Less then Twenty on board our Ship She Stood Down for our Ship these Men Agred one and All that itt was the *Harlem* Privatear from New York.

Now we Got under Way I Made the Nantucket Men an Offer to Sheair All Equal A Like for I Shoud take her; out of the 20 I think thare was Tew Stood by us we Stood for Each Other and before we Gool up with her we Discoverd her to be the Sloop *Providence* that we had parted with of[f] Abaco As we Pased her we ware Rejoiced to See them we had not time to Drar our Shot and we Gave them A Salute and tha [they] Returnd in the Same Maner we hove About and followed the Sloop in; the Wind Moderrates Run under Nantucket and we Came to Anker as the Wind would not Admit of Going over the Shouels.

This is the 20 of feb^r. 1778 A Light are of Wind att N. East and Lukes Lik[e] A Storm Runing by the Round Shoule the Snow begins to fly Quick & the blow Encreses; now a Snow Storm and So thik we can not See but a Short Distanc Runing for Cape Poge About 12 A clock our Ship Struck very hard on a Shole Neair the Horse Shue. We had Very hard Time. A Considerabel of a Sea, we Kept All Sail on her until we Got Acrost the Shole and Depened our warter, and then we Lett go our Anker but Before we Goot of[f] this Shoul We Lost our Ruder and Stove our Boat on Deck.

The Next Morning [21 Feb.] we found the Sloop *Providence* Gatt on Shore Going into Old Town but Sune Got of[f] Again the Next Day by the Asistance of Boats. We Got Safe into Old Town thare we Discharged our Cargo Consisting of Rum Molase[s] Sugers, Corfea, Some Indego & Cotton — a Valuabel Cargo. Some part of our Cargo Sent Down to Hieanners [Hyannis] Some to Boston but the most Sent to Bedford. So Ends this Cruse — (n.11-395)

February 23, 1778, Falmouth

Extract From Freeman,
***History of Cape Cod, Annals of Barnstable County* (1858)**

A company of men was ordered to be raised and stationed at Falmouth, Feb. 23; and the sheriff was directed "to take with him a sufficient force and go to the island of Cuttyhunk and arrest persons engaged in aiding and secreting certain Tories, and in sending provisions to the enemy." (f.I-522)

March 3, 1778

News From New London, Connecticut
Maryland Journal, and the Baltimore Advertiser, March 3, 1778
New London, January 23

By a gentleman just arrived from Bedford, we learn that a sloop of 14 guns [*Haerlem*] has been sent from Newport to Martha's vineyard, to demand pilots for the fleet destined for Boston, to take in Burgoyne's troops; they refused to comply with the demand, and the sloop (after taking a coasting vessel out of Holmes's Hole [*Sally*]) sailed for Newport, it is said, to bring force sufficient to lay waste the island. (n.11-193)

March 8, 1778, Whitehall

Lord George Germain to Lieutenant General Sir Henry Clinton
<u>Most secret</u>

Sir,
    In my Letter to you of the 4th. of February I acquainted you that, Sir William Howe having requested His Majesty's Permission to resign his Command, His Majesty had been graciously pleased to acquiesce in his Request, and that I had signified to him His Majesty's Pleasure that he should deliver up the Command to you, and put into your Possession all Orders & Instructions he has received from me, or any other of the King's Servants respecting the Troops, or the Operations in which they have been, or were to be employed. The devolution of so great a Trust would, upon any Occasion, carry with it the highest Proof of the Royal Confidence; but, in the present Circumstances, when the most essential Interests of the British Empire are so deeply engaged, and the Power, Reputation, and future Welfare of this Nation depend, in so great a degree, upon the Successful Employment of the Forces committed to your Command, the Importance of the trust increases with the Immensity of the Object, and is the fullest Manifestation of His Majesty's entire Reliance upon your Zeal & Ability.
    ...It is therefore recommended to you, if you should find it impracticable to bring Mr. Washington to a general and decisive Action early in the Campaign, to relinquish the Idea of carrying on

offensive Operations against the Rebels within Land, and, as soon as the Season will permit, to embark such a Body of Troops as can be spared from the Defence of the Posts you may think necessary to maintain, on board of transports under the Conduct of a proper number of the King's Ships with Orders to attack the Ports on the Coast, from New York to Nova Scotia, and to Seize or destroy every Ship or Vessel in the different Creeks or Harbours, wherever it is found practicable to penetrate; as also to destroy all Wharfs and Stores, and Materials for Ship-building, so as to incapacitate them from raising a Marine, or continuing their Depredations upon the Trade of this Kingdom, which has been already so much annoyed by their Ships of War and Privateers. This Service, it is imagined, will best be executed by two different Armaments; The principal One to Set out from New York, and the Other from Halifax; that, while the Connecticut Coast is attacked on the one Side, the like Attempts may be made on the Ports in the Province of Maine and New Hampshire on the Other, and both Armaments unite, or act in Concert, for the Attack of Boston, and the other Ports in the Massachuset's Bay: And it may be hoped that the Troops & Ships at Rhode Island will find a favorable Opportunity, while these Operations are carrying on, to destroy the Shipping in Providence River, & those in the other Creeks, which branch out of Rhode Island Harbour. The number of Troops & Ships necessary for this Service must be left to you and the Admiral to determine; but I am commanded to say to you, that the Object appears to the King of such Importance, that should you be of Opinion a number of Troops, sufficient to ensure Success in the different Enterprises, cannot be spared with Safety to Philadelphia, it is His Majesty's Pleasure that you do consult with the Admiral upon the most proper Situation for establishing a Post upon the Delaware River, if you shall think a Post upon that River necessary, capable of being defended by a small Body of Men, and of giving Protection to the Ships, which it may be necessary to station in that River, and that, when you shall have taken such Measures as you and the Admiral shall judge necessary and effectual, for obstructing the Navigation of the River by the Rebels, you do withdraw the Troops from Philadelphia, and, leaving a sufficient Garrison in the Post you may have established, embark the rest, and proceed to New York, with such part as you shall not think necessary for the Service abovementioned. I would not however be understood to convey it to you as His Majesty's Opinion that the Possession of Philadelphia is an Object of small Importance, on the contrary His Majesty conceives the Possession of it may be attended with many Advantages, & that the abandoning it may be productive of some ill Consequences, and therefore it is His Majesty's Wish that you may be able to retain it, and He consents to your withdrawing from it only upon the Supposition that the Service I have been pointing out to you, cannot, in your Opinion, be effected while it is retained. When these Operations on the Sea Coasts of the Northern Provinces are concluded, which it is supposed they will be before the Month of October, it is the King's Intention that an Attack should be made upon the Southern Colonies with a View to the Conquest and Possession of Georgia & South Carolina.... (n.11-1069)

May 3, 1778, Sandwich

Joseph Nye to Council of the State of the Massachusetts Bay [?]

May it please your Hon[s]

Lieut. Fish who commands the Guard on The Elizabeth I. has this moment informed me of the following disagreable piece of intelligence. Viz; On the 1st. instant one of the Enemies ships and two or three armed Vessels arrived there and made a demand of the Stock on sd Island upon being refused landed a party of men and were Collecting the Sheep on one of the Outer Islands in order to [carry them] off as this was the very day the five men's time expired, who were stationed there, and after having sent in vain for assistance from the Militia of Falmouth, he was put to the disagreable Necessity of Abandoning the Fort, after removing Everything in it but the Cannon and as there is now no force upon the Island, the Enemy will undoubtly effect their design; he desires me further to inform your Hon[rs] that at the time of the Enemies landing he had but five men with him One of whom had just broke out with the Small Pox and as he finds it impossible to engage a sufficient number of men to defend sd. Island. Begs your Honors to dismiss him from the Service & to take such Order thereon as you in your wisdom shall think fit.

I remain Yr. Hon. most Obt. Servant

Joseph Nye (e.281)

May 5, 1778, Narragansett Bay

Diary of Lt. Colonel Friederich Von der Malsburg [?]
Hessian Regiment Von Ditfurth

At five o'clock in the morning, the weather being very fine and the wind west northwest, the fleet set sail; we followed the sloop *Harlem*, a transport and four small vessels followed us, and the *Sphynx*, a 20 gun ship, brought up the rear, the sloop having fourteen guns. About 8 o'clock the Beaver Taillight was passed, and when we reached the open sea the captain (of the *Sphynx*) opened the orders, from which we found we were to sail to the Elizabeth islands in Massasuchets. As we passed the eastern coast of Rhode Island there met us six ships from New York under convoy of the frigate *Swan*.

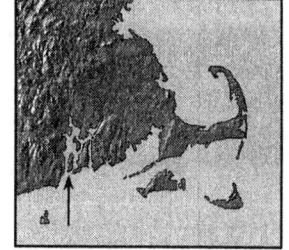

Towards 11 we saw the point of Ponny Ganset and the town of Bedford, where were some boats. About one we passed the islands Cuttehank, Pennakeas, Nashawinna, Peshtemet, Nawshon and Nonnamiset. Here we saw a large ship, and with the idea that it was an enemy we prepared for action, but when we came nearer we found that it was the frigate *Union*, which, awaiting us lay at anchor here. The wind was now contrary, yet we kept on, and at 2 passed the *Union*. Her Commander, Captain Ford, now our commodore, advised us in passing, since the wind was so unfavorable, to come to anchor. Nevertheless we cruised about in Puxaurds [Buzzards] Bay and when opposite [New] Bedford we came too near a hostile battery, and they fired on us; the distance was too great, however, for them to injure us; and then we heard in the neighborhood many alarm shots. In the evening at 7 o'clock we came to anchor off Nawshon. Captain Coore of the British Grenadiers informed us that we should land on this island at six o'clock in the morning....

May 6, 1778, Off Naushon in Buzzards Bay

...The sentry on deck reported this morning that he had seen various fires during the night on the island, which made us think that we might perhaps meet a powerful enemy. At six o'clock a signal was given to set sail. We cruised along the island to the western side, where the frigates *Union* and *Sphynx* and the sloop *Harlem* lay at anchor; here we anchored also, whilst the armed sloop guarded the eastern side.

At half past seven, the commodore sent for the captains of the transports, who at their return brought with them the orders that in case of necessity the sailors should be armed to fight with us. These orders were immediately made known to them. At eight the signal was given for landing, and the boats were launched.

Meanwhile a man with a white flag appeared upon the shore and was taken by one of the boats of the *Sphynx* to the commodore. He brought the news that the enemy, 150 in number, had left the island a week before, at which time the news of our expedition had reached them. He, together with three others,  were the inhabitants of this island. These were tenants of Mr Ried, a member of the Congress at Boston, but his farm, with everything upon it was his own. Through the whole war he had been, as a Quaker, a friend of the government, and, accordingly, commended himself to his Majesty's grace and our protection. On this the man whose name was Robisson, was sent to shore and we landed immediately after.

As soon as we had landed the chasseurs were deployed on both wings, I having the right and Lieutenant Murarius the left wing, and the flank company being in the center. Each company had detailed twenty men, who left their weapons on shipboard, to drive the cattle behind us. In this manner the troops stretched across the island, which is perhaps an hour (about two miles) in breadth, and marched through undergrowth and woods about 9 English miles, the length of the island. In the middle of this, opposite the Island of Martha's Vineyard, which is separated from this island by a channel two miles broad, we found two batteries, the one with two and the other with three twelve pounders.

As we approached, an inhabitant came towards us whose house was not far off. He held a white cloth fastened on a stick as a sign of friendship in his hand, and had a little girl of perhaps eight years with him, who held in her left hand an egg as a token of confidence and innocence; and on our accepting this held out the right with a kiss. He commended himself as a friend of his king to my protection, which I promised him. Near this battery were barracks for three hundred men built, and not far from this were two other buildings in which were some casks of the finest powder and salt which the enemy had manufactured on the island, and which were immediately burned. A house standing nearby, in which a man lay sick with the smallpox, an attendant being with him was left untouched. All the captured cattle were driven to a meadow to the west of this battery and left under a guard.

We followed our course to the extreme eastern point of the island, where the previously mentioned Robisson had his house. Nashavinna lies on the opposite side of the channel. Here we came across some deer in the undergrowth, and a corporal of my company shot one of them. By four o'clock in the afternoon the island had been thoroughly searched without meeting an enemy. We officers dined at the house of Robisson, and in the evening went on board ship with our soldiers [at] Aliquumvisit, a harbor not far from Falmouth to the southeast of this island, a ship of 300 tons was burned by the sloop *Harlem*....

May 7, 1778, Off Naushon in Buzzards Bay

...At seven o'clock the commodore gave the signal for the landing again of the troops. We landed an hour after at the southern point of the island, where yesterday the frigates and transports had laid at anchor. Lieutenant Murarius was detailed with some chasseurs and some of the flank companies to drive the cattle to Robisson's house. The flank companies meanwhile traversed the island once more in order to drive in any cattle which had been overlooked, and I was rowed over to Pesktenset. At my return, Lieutenant Murarius came with the cattle to the designated place, and the boats being prepared for shipping, the sheep were first taken on board.

At 4 P.M. the flank companies returned without any more cattle. I dined on board the *Union*. In the evening after all the sheep, 900 in number, had been shipped, the troops went on board...

May 8, 1778, Off Naushon in Buzzards Bay

...With the break of day a signal was made to ship the cattle of which there were 80, and having finished the task by 9 o'clock, we set sail at 10 o'clock in a thick fog under convoy of the frigate *Sphynx* for Rhode Island. (e.284-287)

Nathaniel Freeman to the Council
Dated at Falmouth May 8, 1778

To the Hon. Council of the State of Massachusetts Bay

May it please your Honors to indulge me in giving you a narration of difficult and alarming situation of this County. The drain of our men for sd. Land service hath been equal in proportion to perhaps any other County in the State, as I believe we have as nearly completed our quota of Sd Continental Army, our supply of men to sd Navy hath been very large we have a considerable Number who have been taken on [ ] voyages etc. Some have gone off & joined the enemy.

We have many remaining whose principles and conduct is unfriendly. We are but a strip of sand almost surrounded by the sea and several commodious harbours on our shores within which the enemys ship & Tenders have been frequently of late particularly at the mouth of Hianis, in the Vineyard Sound, at Tarpolin Cove in Buzzards Bay etc. They have been sounding our Harbours, and up Buzzards Bay & Warham river.

The 6th. Inst. we had notice from Warham that Gen. Sullivan had sent word that a number of sd. troops had embarked at Newport & come this way. We were likewise informed that 4 ships and several tenders lay at the mouth of Bedford River and it was supposed they were designed to destroy that town. That the militia from Warham had marched to and upon this I ordered sd. whole Regiment to be mustered & in readiness to march to any place that should be attacked. In the evening rec'd. intelligence that about 13 sail were seen crossing the Bay from Bedford towards Elizabeth Island, supposed to be on a sheep stealing expedition.

Our militia at Sandwich were got together in due course that night and to their honor turned out cheerfully & generally, and next morning receiving intelligence marched them to Falmouth which lies about 18 miles distance from any neighboring town & from Sandwich, we apprehending the designs of the enemy were to strip the Islands of the Stock & destroy the salt works along the shoar, as we have undoubted accounts they have accomplished & in some places westward (executed) and perhaps of their burning some houses in Falmouth.

When we arrived at Falmouth we found that 16 or 17 sail of men of war, Transports & Tenders were at Quixes Hole & round the Island, that they landed 400 men and were taking off the Stock. We had about 200 of the militia and had it in contemplation to go on upon the Island & prevent their taking the Stock etc. but we sent on upon Nonnamessett Island and obtained the following intelligence, Viz; that they landed 1000 or 800 men at least upon the Island and drove all off from one end to the other, both sheep, cattle, horses, poultry some Venison and had got most or all aboard, and if not, had got them in Pound at the West End of the Island, but that it was supposed they were aboard & the most the sd fleet sailed for Newport. That they had burned the new and old Barracks, robb'd. the few inhabitants of considerable of their household stuff, carried off a quantity of Barrelled Beef that belonged to Mr. Read taken Mr. John Nye; and that Capt. Nye who kept upon sd [skulking] in the wood was shot at 3 times and once or twice by his Townsman Perry who had joined the Enemy; that Perry's vessel & Bowin's [?] vessel (both went from Sandwich) were in the fleet; that one Tupper who went from Sandwich likewise was very [busy] and full of [ ].

Upon receiving this intelligence and finding we could procure only 2 boats to go on with and there remaining no prospect of their committing any further ravages at this time, we discharged the militia. But we soon expect another visit from them as they were heard to say it was intended to destroy ye salt-works & they should return. Under all these difficulties your Hon. must be sensible it would be extremely injurious for us to send a number of our men away from defending their own towns and properties, in immediate danger, to guard the coast in other places, in another State. We are obliged to keep up watches every Night for an extent of 50 miles at every inlet. I therefore entreat your Hon. that 70 men raised for ye State of Rhode Island may be stationed in this

County or at ye Island if it be found anything remains worth defending, or at Falmouth as that is now become a frontier.

If the people are properly encouraged, I have no doubt they will make a resolute stand before they would surrender any part of ye County, but if not, I really fear ye same spirit of Neutrality that hath in some measure taken place at the Vineyard will possess the minds of some part of this County, infested with so many Tories. I beg your honors would give some directions relative hereto & Oblige yr. Hon. most Obt. Servant.

N. Freeman

P.S. I forgot to mention that ye evening before we go to Falmouth the enemy sent a party to Woods Hole & burned ye Prize ship that lay within 100 yds. of the shoar. (e.289)

Vice Admiral Richard, Lord Howe, R. N.

Major John André, Adjutant to General Clinton.
"He was the Handsomest Man I ever laid eyes on." (a)

8
Grey's Raid on Martha's Vineyard

"Major [John] André was executed [as a spy] at Tappan on the second of October, 1780...His Breakfast being sent to him from the table of George Washington, which had been done every day of his confinement, he partook of it as usual, and having shaved and dressed himself, he placed his hat on the table, and cheerfully said to the guard officers: "I am ready at any moment, gentlemen, to wait on you." The fatal hour having arrived, a large detachment of troops was paraded and an immense concourse of people assembled. Almost all our general and field-officers, excepting his Excellency [Washington], were present on horseback. Melancholy and gloom pervaded all ranks, and the scene was awfully affecting"...Dr. Thacher (a)

"Never did a man suffer death with more justice, or deserve it less. There was something singularly interesting in the character and fortunes of André. To an excellent understanding, well improved by education and travel, he united a peculiar elegance of mind and manners, and the advantage of a pleasing person"...Alexander Hamilton (a)

Extracts from Major John André's Journal
Operations of the British Army under
Generals Sir William Howe and Sir Henry Clinton
June 1777 to November 1778

September 4, 1778, New London

...At five in the afternoon the Fleet sailed away from New London, and at sunset bore away for the Eastward....

September 5, 1778
Long Island Sound and Buzzards Bay

...At three in the morning, we discovered several sail of large ships. The Commodore in consequence changed his course and stood for Rhode Island. At seven in the morning the strange Fleet came up with us. It consisted of several sail of the Line of Lord Howe's Squadron. Captain Fanshaw went on board Lord Howe's ship. Lord Howe told Captain Fanshaw that he would remain off Block Island until he heard the issue of our Expedition. At eight o' clock the Fleet stood its course again towards Buzzard's Bay with a view to Bedford. The flat boats were hoisted out whilst the transports were under way. The *Carisfort*, in passing thro' the bay struck twice upon the rocks, but got off again immediately.

A little before sunset, the ships reached their stations in Clark's Cove, and the Troops from the transports assembled in the flat boats at Captain Henry's Boat and landed without opposition. The Light Infantry and Grenadiers were the first disembarked, and this was conducted with the greatest rapidity. As soon as the Light Infantry and Grenadiers were landed and the boats returned to fetch the remainder of the Troops, they marched on with all expedition to New Bedford, and six Companies under Sir James Murray were sent into the town to burn the vessels at the wharves, the stores, &c. In the meantime the advanced Corps took post at the entrance of the town and crossroads north of it until, the rest of the Troops being disembarked and at hand, they proceeded to the head of the river (seven miles) and took post on the heights on either side that pass. The burning party, being reinforced by three Companies of the 42d Regiment, proceeded up the banks of the river destroying everything at McPherson's and other wharves.

The 33rd and 64th passed the Grenadiers and Light Infantry at the bridge at the head of the river, and marched a little way down the opposite shore upon the Fair Haven Road. Everything being consumed on the West side of the river, the Troops marched down the other shore, and in passing Fair Haven, the 33rd entered that place and destroyed everything of stores and shipping, falling afterwards in the rear of the Column. This was to proceed to Skonticut Neck, a very narrow point of land which juts out opposite to Clark's Neck, from which place the boats and vessels had crossed over to Skonticut to receive it on board when the service should have been performed. Colonel Donkin with the 17th and 44th Regiments, had been landed here and guarded the Isthmus in the meantime. The guide very unaccountably carried us thro' a wrong road which led to a Rebel Battery on a point between Fair Haven and Skonticut Neck, thinking perhaps we might, by going along the beach, gain our place of embarkation.

After destroying the Battery, which we found evacuated, we followed the course of the shore over trackless ground until stopped by a run of water which obliged us to turn to our left to search and fall into the road which headed the run, a detour which brought us back to Fair Haven; from hence we gained the Neck and joined Colonel Donkin at about six in the morning. At twelve General Grey came on board the *Carisfort*, the whole being re-embarked. We had a few men wounded by people lurking in the swamps and behind stone fences, and by a few shots which were fired as the Grenadiers and Light Infantry took possession of the heights near Crane's Mills (the head of the river). The Rebels carried from New Bedford four pieces of brass cannon from which they fired a shot or two as they retired on the Boston Road. A Company of Militia and the Artillery men belonging to those guns were, we heard, the only Troops there. Three or four men of the

Enemy were found bayonetted, one an Officer. They had fired at the advanced party and were not alert enough to get off.

Major General Grey determined to proceed from thence to Martha's Vineyard, and wrote to Sir Robert Pigot at Rhode Island to desire he would send vessels to receive cattle.

September 7, 1778, Buzzards Bay

...The Fleet got under way this morning, but the wind failing, came to an anchor at 11 o'clock, when a boat from the town came on board with a letter from a Rebel Major proposing an exchange of prisoners; to which General Grey consented, provided the men of ours in their hands were brought on board before the Fleet sailed. They were not brought.

At 1 o'clock two of the Gallies with some armed boats under the command of Captain Browne of the *Scorpion*, and four Light Infantry Companies under Captain Baillie put off from the Fleet to destroy a large vessel on the stocks on Aponeganset Neck, which service they effected. They received a few shot from the shore on their return.

At 10 o'clock at night the *Cornwallis* and *Dependence* Gallies with some armed boats, destroyed two large schooners which lay in the Harbour near Fair Haven. It was not executed without receiving a heavy fire of musketry from the shore. The Lieutenant of the *Fowey* and one seaman were wounded.

September 8, 1778, Quick's Hole

...The Fleet got under way at noon. The General was obliged to reduce the allowance of provisions to two-thirds. Came to an anchor about two leagues from Quickso's Hole.

September 9, 1778, Quick's Hole

...Sailed at 7 in the morning. The ships could not all get thro' the Hole before the tide turned.

September 10, 1778, Holmes Hole

...The Fleet weighed anchor at 6 in the morning and turned thro' the Vineyard Sound, passing Tarpaulin Cove, Wood's Hole Harbour and Falmouth. The gallies went into the last place and cut out two sloops and a schooner, and burned another vessel. At 1 o'clock the *Carisfort* came to an anchor off Holmes Hole. The transports and small vessels were ordered into the Harbour, excepting those which carried the Grenadiers and Light Infantry and 33rd Regiment, which Troops General Grey intended taking with him to Nantucket.

General Grey's proposal to Captain Fanshaw was in the following words:

> *Carisfort,* 9th Set. 1778 Major-General Grey proposes to Captain Fanshaw that whilst part of the troops and ships are employed in destroying the Rebel vessels which may be found at Falmouth, Barker's Harbour [Parker's Harbor?, i.e. Little Harbor?] and Wood's Hole Harbour and in procuring the necessary refreshments from Martha's Vineyard, that a body of Troops with such of the Men-of-War and gallies as he shall think proper, be detached without delay to Nantucket Island, which is one of the most noted resorts of Privateers in America, the destruction of which must be thought of infinite service.
>
> The pilots inform him that the distance is not more than three hours from Holmes's Hole, that the ships can anchor perfectly secure within half a mile of Nantucket Cliff, where it is proposed to land the troops, who will proceed to the town, which is two miles distant, attended by the gallies, and there destroy or secure such vessels and stores as may be found; the former are supposed to amount, from the accounts of the different pilots, to 200 sail, and on the bar they agree there is nine feet water.

To this Captain Fanshaw made the following reply:

> Captain Fanshaw is ready to proceed with the King's ships and transports under his Order, according to Major-General Grey's proposal. Captain Fanshaw wishes generally throughout the course of service on which the Fleet is employed, to have it

understood that he has not an opinion to offer on the propriety of any movement; but will always endeavour to promote whatever may be required for the King's service.

R. FANSHAW

General Grey wished Captain Fanshaw to proceed on the Nantucket service without coming to an anchor off Holmes's Hole Harbour, as the wind was fair; but Captain Fanshaw insisting on the necessity of assembling his Captains, the deliberation lasted until the wind changed.

In the evening a Flag of Truce with three Committeemen came on board. They professed the most peaceable dispositions and the utmost readiness to comply with the General's requisitions. General Grey ordered them ashore to direct the inhabitants to drive in their sheep and cattle, or that Troops should be marched thro' the Island; likewise to bring in their arms, or that the Colonel and Captains of the Militia should be sent prisoners to New York.

Captain Robert Fanshaw, R. N., c.1770.

September 11, 1778, Holmes Hole

...A detachment of 150 men from each of the Corps in the Harbour disembarked under Lieutenant Colonel Stirling. He consented not to march into the country provided the inhabitants should immediately furnish 10,000 sheep and 300 oxen, with hay for them. Twenty vessels from Rhode Island arrived to take in stock.

September 12, 1778, Holmes Hole

...Wind unfavorable for Nantucket. A quantity of stock was embarked for Rhode Island, and the vessels sailed. The 17th, 37th and 46th Regiments (The 150 men from each of the corps are here alluded to) were ordered from their different positions to the beach. The 44th under Colonel Donkin, marched towards the Southeast of the Island. Only 229 stand of arms having been brought in, the Colonel and five Captains were confined. The Committeemen were likewise confined for having concealed a quantity of ammunition.

September 13, 1778, Holmes Hole

...The 17th, 37th and 46th Regiments embarked. More arms, sheep and oxen were brought in. Two men having deserted, the inhabitants were required to restore them, on pain of having a double number of their friends seized. A Tender arrived from Lord Howe with Orders to the Fleet to return to New York. The Nantucket Expedition was of course set aside.

The cattle and sheep were embarked on board the Men-of-War and transports. Colonel Donkin was ordered to return from Chilmarck.

September 14, 1778, Holmes Hole

...The remainder of the cattle was embarked. The Troops embarked. The deserters were restored and the Militia officers and Committeemen released, with a solemn injunction to abstain from taking part any more in the War or persecuting others for their political opinions; they were also bound to assist the King's ships with water or provisions whenever they should call upon them to do it. The public money which had been required, was paid, being a tax just collected by authority of the Congress. A salt work was destroyed this day.

September 15, 1778, Holmes Hole

...The signal was made for sailing at 6 in the morning, but the transports were so dilatory that it was sunset before they came up with the Commodore. The whole sailed. A schooner and sloop taken in Holmes's Hole Harbour were burnt. (a.87-93)

September 18, 1778, Whitestone

General Grey's Report to Sir Henry Clinton
Clarisfort, off Whitestone Sept. 18, 1778

Sir:
    In the evening of the 4th inst. the Fleet with the detachment under my command sailed from New London and stood to the Eastward with a very favourable wind. We were only retarded in the run from thence to Buzzard's Bay, by altering our course for some hours in the night in consequence of our discovering a strange Fleet, which was not known to be Lord Howe's until morning. By 5 o'clock in the afternoon of the 5th the ships were at anchor in Clark's Cove, and the boats having been previously hoisted out, the debarkation of the Troops took place immediately. I proceeded without loss of time to destroy the vessels and stores in the whole extent of Acushnet River (about seven miles) particularly at Fair Haven and Bedford, and having dismantled and burnt a fort mounting eleven guns, with a magazine and barracks for the east side of the River, completed the re-embarkation before noon the next day. I refer your Excellency to the annexed Returns for the damage done the Enemy, as well as we could ascertain it, and for our own casualties.
    The wind did not admit of any further movements of the Fleet on the 6th and 7th, than hauling a little distance from the shore. Advantage was taken of these circumstances to burn a large Privateer ship on the stocks, and to send a small armament of boats with two galleys to destroy a vessel or two, which being in the stream, the Troops had not been able to set fire to. From the

difficulties in passing out of Buzzard's Bay into the Vineyard Sound, thro' Quickso's Hole, and from head winds, the Fleet did not reach Holmes's Hole Harbour in the Island of Martha's Vineyard until the 10th. The transports with the Light Infantry, Grenadiers and 88d Regiment were anchored without the Harbour, as I had at that time a service in view for those Corps whilst the business of collecting cattle should be carrying on upon the island. Contrary winds obliged me to relinquish my designs.

On our arrival off the Harbour the inhabitants sent persons on board to ask my intentions with respect to them, to which a Requisition was made of-

The arms of the Militia
The Public Money
Three hundred oxen and 10,000 sheep

They promised each of these articles should be delivered without delay. I afterwards found it necessary to send small detachments into the island and detain the deputed inhabitants for a time to accelerate their compliance with the demand. On the 12th I was able to embark on board the vessels which arrived that day from Rhode Island, 6000 sheep and 180 oxen.

The 18th and 14th were employed in embarking cattle and sheep on board our own Fleet; in destroying some salt works; in burning or taking in the inlets what vessels or boats could be found, and in recovering the arms of the Militia. I here again refer your Excellency to the Returns.

On the 15th the Fleet left Martha's Vineyard, and after sustaining the next day a very severe gale of wind, arrived the 17th at Whitestone without any material damage. I consider myself much obliged to the Commanding Officers of Corps, and the Troops in general for the alacrity with which every service was performed.

I have the honour, etc.

Account of Vessels and Stores Destroyed in Acushnet River the 5th

Eight Sail of large vessels from 200 to 300 ton burthen, mostly prizes, three taken by the French.

Six Armed Vessels carrying from sixteen to ten (changed in original copy from eighteen) guns, a number of sloops and schooners amounting in all to about seventy sail, inclusive of whale boats and other small craft. Twenty-six store houses at New Bedford, several at Fair Haven, or at McPherson's Wharf and Crane's Mills. These were filled (as well as some private houses which were consumed) with great quantities of rum, sugar, molasses, coffee, tea, tobacco, medicines, cotton, gunpowder, sail-cloth, cordage, &c. Two large rope-walks, at Falmouth in the Vineyard Sound the 10th. Brought away by the galley, two sloops and a schooner, one loaded with staves, &c. Burnt one sloop in Old Town Harbour, Martha's Vineyard; burnt by the *Scorpion*, a brig, 150 ton, a schooner, seventy ton, a sloop and 23 whaleboats taken or destroyed; a quantity of plank brought off at Holmes's Hole. Four vessels with several boats taken or destroyed; a salt-work destroyed.

Arms and Ammunition at Martha's Vineyard

Forty-nine bayonets, seventy-seven pouches, twenty-five swords, four pistols, one drum, powder, flints and leaden balls. In Acushnet River thirteen pieces of iron ordnance, a quantity of powder blown up, barracks for 200 men burnt. Martha's Vineyard, 10,000 sheep, 300 cattle and £950 Continental currency, a tax levied by ye Congress.

Return of Killed, Wounded and Missing at Bedford in Buzzard's Bay, 7th September, 1778

Regiment	Killed	Wounded	Missing
Light Infantry	1	2	3
Grenadiers	-	1	3
33d .	-	-	1
42d .	-	1	8
46th .	-	-	1
64th .	-	1	-
Totals	1	4	16

Five men of the 42nd came in afterward, having made their escape. (a.94-97)

Extract from Freeman, *History of Cape Cod, Annals of Falmouth* (1862)

The attempt of the enemy on this town, Sept 10, was not unanticipated. The Tories in this region had more than intimated such demonstration; and the operations of the enemy at Fairhaven and New Bedford on the 5th had sufficiently forewarned the inhabitants of this town that the jubilant aspect of sympathizers with the British was not without cause. Refugees were known to be near by, assisting in the marauding excursions to the island, and ready to act as guides in the contemplated grand attack. The entire militia of the neighboring towns were called out. Their interposition was, however, soon found to be unnecessary. The enemy, after burning one coaster, and cutting out four others that were sent for safety to a harbor four miles distant [Waquoit?] – an act consummated before the militia could reach there, – confined their operations to depredations at the Vineyard, carrying off many thousand sheep, hundreds of cattle, many arms and accoutrements, – all that could be collected, all the corn and vegetables that could be found, burning a brig, with several smaller vessels, and numerous boats, and seizing the public moneys. They even opened newly-made graves, so intent were they in search of treasure, rifled private dwellings, and ruthlessly broke the windows. They then, on the 15th, moved westward. (f.II-453)

Captain Robert Fanshaw to Lord George Germain
Clarisfort; off Bedford, Sept. 6, 1778

My Lord:
I enclose to your lordship a copy of Rear-Admiral Gambier's order to proceed with a detachment of ships and transports and assist in such services as His Excy. Sir H. Clinton, or Maj, Gen. Grey, should propose. Last evening, the fleet came before Bedford harbor. I send your lordship an outline sketch of the scene of

operation, and the plan and execution of the naval part with minutes of the manner in which it was performed. I am informed that the army in its progress destroyed all the stores, wharves, and shipping at them; two or three sloops only, by being on float. escaped the flames...It is with great pleasure I hear that the army has had very little loss. The enemy, not expecting an attack, was not prepared to resist. I cannot particularize the damage done; but by the appearance of the shipping before dark, and the conflagration, I suppose it must be very great...Prisoners report 70 sail destroyed, of which eight were large ships laden, and four privateers; great quantities of canvas, cordage, pitch, turpentine, tobacco, coffee, etc.... (f.II-453)

Extract from Freeman,
***History of Cape Cod, Annals of Falmouth* (1862)**

...We here remark, [the] report of Com. Fanshaw conflicts somewhat with contemporaneous accounts; for instance, the suppression of the fact of the burning of dwellings, barns, mills, etc., on the march through New Bedford, Acushnet, and around Oxford and Fairhaven to Sconticut Neck, where they encamped 4000 strong; and that persons were wantonly shot by soldiers *en route*. The fleet from which this large body of troops landed consisted of 32 vessels, the largest ship or 40 guns,- the Careysport [*Clarisfort*], on board which was Gen. Grey, the military commander of the expedition. The design, doubtless, was to finish the work of destruction in Bristol County by burning Fairhaven the following night; but the militia from the neighboring towns were, by this time, on hand, and although a large body of Br. troops proceeded up the river, firing buildings on their way, they met now with an unexpectedly warm reception.

To Brig. Gen. Fearing, then a Major, from Wareham, has been awarded distinguished honor for prompt decision and bravery on this occasion. He had only about 110 men with him, whose well-directed fire took the enemy so completely by surprise that they quickly retreated to their ships. It is remarkable that, in all attempts made in these parts by the enemy, they seem to have been, whenever resisted, impressed with the idea that they were encountering superior numbers.... (f.II-453)

October 31, 1778, London
William Knox [Secretary to Lord Germain] to General Sullivan [in Newport]

What a proof is the Bedford enterprize of the propriety of the orders so repeatedly given for attacking the rebel sea ports, and what a reflection is it upon Lord Howe's character that Gambier, in his short absence, has done more to subdue the Rebellion than his lordship during the whole of his command. It was always clear in speculation that the Militia would never stay with Washington or quit their homes, if the coast was kept in alarm, but the experiment having now been made, the effect is reduced to a certainty. Surely somebody will ask Lord Howe why he has never attempted anything of the kind. I much fear [D'Estaing] will go to the West Indies, ...but perhaps Byron's enterprizing turn may discover the practicability of burning his fleet and the town of Boston together, and then everything will succeed with us. (k.1-334)

Brig with Wind Abeam.

9

Falmouth Threatened

The Kings' American Regiment [KAR]

While the [King's American] regiment remained mostly idle that winter [1778-1779], another group of Loyalists made their presence felt in Newport. George LEONARD, a wealthy Massachusetts Loyalist and one of the refugees from Boston in 1776, devised a plan to operate a fleet of both privateers and transport ships, manned with Loyalist sailors and carrying armed Loyalist refugees on board, to raid the New England coast.

While LEONARD provided the capital, he used people like Edmund FANNING and Edward WINSLOW to organize the land component of his new group, called the Loyal Associated Refugees. This group was not a Provincial regiment and therefore did not receive pay or uniform clothing. They did draw arms and ordnance stores from the government, but little more than that.

However, they were instrumental in providing the garrison with cattle, provisions and firewood, taking it from the Rebels and paying for it from Loyalists. Their boldest excursion was to negotiate a supply contract with Martha's Vineyard without any hostilities.

One joint operation between the Provincials and the Refugees took place between 30 March and 6 April 1779 in Bedford (modern New Bedford), Massachusetts. A Detachment consisting of the Grenadier Company of the King's American Regiment under Captain DePEYSTER, twenty seven or more men from the Loyal New Englanders under Lieutenant Richard HOLLAND, and Governor Wentworth's Volunteers under Captain Daniel MURRAY, joined the Refugees, embarking on board transports and the Refugee Privateer *General Leslie* on 31 March 1779.

The detachment was ordered to proceed to Bedford, where they were to occupy the town, destroy all public stores, barracks, store houses, etc. They were to man all the Rebel vessels captured at the wharves or in the harbor, after which they were immediately to return to Newport. DePEYSTER's Company was to be in the front throughout the expedition, as undoubtedly the best troops on the expedition.

The expedition failed due to the wind not allowing the ships to enter the harbor and the Rebels gathering in large numbers to oppose them. They sailed off to Falmouth, where the privateers bombarded the town for two hours. After making a show of landing, they sailed back to Newport, having alarmed a lot of towns, but achieving little else.[5]

Edward Winslow [JR]
From *Sibley's Harvard Graduates*

Judge Edward (Ned) Winslow of New Brunswick [Canada] was born at Plymouth, Massachusetts, on February 20 1746/7, a son of Edward (A.B. 1736) and Hannah (Dyer) Winslow, who in 1754 built the great mansion looking down on Plymouth Rock. Many years later, remembering a childhood in colonial Plymouth, the Judge wrote:

> You know I was born in a land of psalmody. For several years together there was nothing heard but old men and women bawling psalms and young men and maids screeching hymns. There was one old man who was a Teacher and Composer and I remember to have seen him in the very act of composition. He sat by a joint stool with a pen, ink and little book, and between his legs he held a half-grown kitten which he occasionally twigged by the tail or plucked by the ears. I asked what the devil he was about? With wonderful simplicity and gravity he answered that out of her squeeling he might possibly pick up a sound that would assist him in forming a tune.

...Ned later said that Governor Hutchinson had appointed him to form a military company to assist the civil magistrates. Perhaps "encouraged" would have been more accurate. At any rate, he formed and largely supported a company of Tories which kept Plymouth were in extreme confusion." It could not, however, cope

---

[5] http://www.royalprovincial.com/military/rhist/kar/kar5hist.htm

Woods Hole from Nobska, Looking West.

with the excitement created by the Hutchinson address affair, and in October, 1774, Winslow fled to join General Gage at Danbury. Thence he went to Boston, where with Peter Oliver (A.B. 1761) he asked Admiral Graves to send an armed vessel to Plymouth Harbor in order to protect the loyal subjects of the Crown. But it was too late. On the Nineteenth of April he rode with Percy's column to Lexington and Concord, on the retreat "led them to safety from their difficult position across the country to Bunker's Hill," and had a horse shot under him....

...In March, 1779, [his] Muster-Master's duties were considerably expanded. It was obvious that the Loyalist force in Newport known as the Rhode Island Refugees would "go to the devil" unless a demonstration of force was made in their area. So General Vaughan asked Winslow to accept command of an expedition to be directed by Edmund Fanning (Class of 1757) from New York and transported by a fleet commanded by George Leonard of Boston. Typically, Ned asked for no compensation for his expenses as commander.

The instructions of the Loyalist expedition were to "retaliate upon and make reprisal against the inhabitants of the several Provinces in America, in actual rebellion against their Sovereign," and "to wage war upon their inhuman persecutors, and to use every means in their power, to obtain redress and compensation for the indignities and losses they had suffered." In March, 1779, Winslow proceeded to Newport, where he received orders from Fanning to embark the Grenadier Company of the King's American Regiment on Leonard's fleet and make an attack on Bedford. The attempt was made, but contrary winds prevented a landing at Bedford before a greatly superior force of rebels had gathered to greet them, so Winslow dropped down to Falmouth where he cannonaded the town for two hours, then retired, pleased that he had alarmed the whole coast. A similar attempt in May went the same way, and in June he returned the Regulars under his command to New York.

In September, 1779, after consultation with Fanning, Commodore Leonard embarked Governor Wentworth's (A.B. 1755) Volunteers under the command of Colonel Winslow to pacify Martha's Vineyard and Nantucket. While the militia and artillery of Plymouth, Bristol, and Barnstable gathered futilely on the mainland shore, the fleet dropped anchor at Holmes Hole and summoned the inhabitants of the island to send representatives to a conference on the ship *Restoration*. According to their proclamation, the Colonel and Commodore were "solicitous to afford protection and assistance to peaceable and inoffensive Men" and "as Industrious to punish the refractory and rebellious," and to this end proposed "to consult and agree on such measures as may Conduce to the Safety and advantage of the Inhabitants...as may be consistent with our duty." In the conference, Winslow made the point that the inhabitants ought not to continue to pay taxes to the rebel government in Massachusetts, and apparently the authorities of the State agreed to the extent of granting a temporary remission. On the whole, the Colonel did his best to conciliate the people of the Vineyard, and was well received by them. There were some clashes with the young men which he described as "a specimen of that duplicity and mean evasion which are the distinguishing characteristic of the people of this country." "Your apology," he told the Selectmen,

> we consider...an insult offered to our understandings and as a trick too frequently played in America to pass current at present. The blame of the proceeding is lay'd on "lads" who are supposed to have done the mischief without orders and of course the Town is not answerable, and in imitation of that metropolis of mobs, Boston, you resolve and vote that your are perfectly peaceable, that you disavow all hostile proceedings!

During the summer of 1779 the navy of the Associated Loyalists captured numerous small vessels, and the sale of the prizes and plunder brought in £23,400. Ned had, all along, been sending what money he could scrape up to ease the lot of his father and sister in Plymouth, and to other Massachusetts Loyalists. When one of these, William Apthorp (Class of 1766), was jailed in Boston for passing Continental bills from this source on the ground that they were counterfeit, the Colonel protested bitterly that he had had the money carefully checked for genuineness before sending it. More distressing to the Winslow family was that after the Falmouth action, a Boston newspaper had reported "that Edward Winslow (formerly of Plymouth) was commanding officer when at Falmouth, but being wounded by a ball through the breast, was gone to Newport...although George Leonard (formerly of Boston, Miller) pretended that he was gone to Rhode-Island with the gout in his stomach." By an appeal to General John Sullivan (Class of 1758), the elder Edward Winslow received permission to proceed by cartel to a reunion with his son at Prudence Island in Narragansett Bay on June 13, 1779. As the Colonel's boat approached the rendezvous, he saw his father sitting on the shore:

> In his pocket were papers giving a particular account of my death and burial, etc. As I approached the shore he pulled...the paper from his pocket—looked at it—looked at me; then he cried, "My God, he died!" When I landed—sound and strong, my father fell on his face. I should have deserved everlasting damnation if I could have spoken a word. No, no, I boast, I glory, that I could not speak. I flung myself by my father on the ground: it was his business to begin... "I am glad, I am glad," says he, "to see you my boy," and down he fell.... There were present rebel officers and rebel soldiers, King's officers and King's soldiers, sailors of both denominations and negroes.... All formalities usual with flags was forgotten, every man turned from us, walked different ways and were profoundly silent.[6]

April 1, 1779, Woods Hole

Extracts from Freeman,
***History of Cape Cod, Annals of Falmouth* (1862)**

...a marauding party from the fleet now lying at Tarpaulin Cove, eluding the vigilance of our watch, landed from their boats, having a refugee for their conductor, and proceeded from Woods Hole to the farms of Messrs. Ephraim and Manassah Swift. They drove off 12 head of cattle, knocked them on the head at the beach, and were in the act of taking the carcasses on board, when surprised. The refugees who acted as guides knew that the Swifts kept fine dairies; and the officers had determined on the possession of a good supply of fresh butter and rich cheeses;

---

[6] http://www.lib.unb.ca/winslow/sibley.html#20b

therefore, whilst the main body were robbing stalls, pigsties and hen-roosts, a party entered one of the houses.

Mrs. Manassah Swift was alone with her children; but, meeting the soldiers at the door she demanded if they had a commander? One stepping forward and claiming that he had the honor to command, she replied, "My house is defended by no man, and I have the right to presume that you are a gentleman who will not molest a helpless woman and her children?"

The officer politely inquired if she had any cheese? "Yes," she replied; "but no more than for my own use." He professed a Willingness to buy, but she had none to *sell*. A *refugee*, who made one of the party, then led two of the soldiers to her cheese-room, and each pierced a cheese with his bayonet, expecting to bear them off without further parley; but Mrs. S. confronted them at the door grasped, and slipped her cheeses from their impalement, and bestowed them in her blue-checked apron. "You're a valiant set of fellows, to be sure!"

She was not resisted; the enemy cowed, and, under a properly directed volley of wholesome advice retreated to join their comrades on the beach who were beginning to load the boat with the carcasses of the good woman's milch cows. Returning to the fleet, it was decided to move forward next day and burn the town.

April 2, 1779 (Friday), Falmouth

...Friday April 2nd. in the afternoon, Major Dimock of this town (Falmouth), was informed that about 10 or 12 vessels were seen in the Sound, steering this way; supposed with a design of plundering and destroying this town. He immediately sent expresses to Sandwich and Barnstable for the militia to come to our assistance. Col. Freeman with Capts. Swift and Fish of Sandwich and their companies, arrived here that night and Saturday morning.

...It is said that the evening of the 2nd. was spent by several of the British Officers in a frolic at the house of one John Slocomb on Pesque Island. Slocomb was a well known Tory. He of course was possessed of all their plans. But as he reflected on their purpose, Tory sympathies gave way, and he secretly dispatched his son down the Islands to cross over to the Hole that night and give warning to the Falmouth people.

English Raid on Woods Hole, April 1, 1779. Franklin L. Gifford, 1930s.

April 3, 1779, Falmouth

...It being then very foggy, part of the enemy's fleet appeared off Woods Hole, to which a part of the militia were ordered and posted there. Soon after, the fog cleared off and several of the vessels appeared against the town, near a low level piece of ground that extends from the shore quite [up] to the houses. There had been a small entrenchment made some years ago upon the edge of the beach, which yet remained. Col. Freeman marched the remainder of the men down to the shore, posting about 50 in said entrenchment and about 30 about 130 rods distant, being the most convenient places for the enemy to land.

At about half past eleven, they formed their fleet, consisting of two schooners and eight sloops, into a line against the two posts, and commenced a very warm fire on our people, with cannon balls, double headed shot, bars of iron, grape shot and small arms, and manned their boats, about 10 in number with about 220 men, having to appearance nearly double that number on board, and made various attempts to land in several places, keeping up a constant fire upon our people, from half past eleven A.M. till half past 5 P.M.

Col. Freeman and Maj. Dimock with about 50 men, defended the entrenchments, and repeatedly challenged them (being within call) to land, which they durst not attempt. Our people 'till now had generally reserved their fire, but being ordered to fire, they soon moved off into the Sound, where they remained quiet until next morning. A party of them in their boats attempted to land at Woods Hole, but about 30 of our men posted there gave them a warm fire, which soon drove them off into the Sound, where they remained quiet until the next morning.

A party of them, in their boats, and the boats went to Nonnamesit, an island near Woods Hole, where they landed and killed the few sheep, cows, and hogs the enemy had before left, and threatened to kill the family that lived there, because, they said, the d--d rebels had been killing them. They had two wounded men with them. Our people being about to go upon the island, they retreated precipitately to their boats, carrying off only one hog and half a cow that calved the day before. They inquired of the island's people our numbers, and said the rebels fought like devils.

...They fired on Saturday about 500 cannon. Had the intrenchment been given up, the town could not have been saved, their number on Saturday being much superior to ours, and no men came to reinforce the Sandwich and Falmouth men until the firing was over on Saturday. Col. Freeman and Major Dimock with their officers and men behaved with the greatest prudence, resolution, and bravery; and we hope those base enemies of our country will be deterred from future attempts on this town. The weather was favorable to our cause, for although many buildings were struck by the fire of the assailants, the thaw prevented the rebounding of their missiles and but little damage was done. Alarms, however, continued to be frequent.

April 4, 1779, Falmouth

...The next day [Sunday], April 4th, a little after sunrise, they fired again from the vessels to drive us from our intrenchment and our people returned them a warm fire with their small-arms for a few minutes, upon which they put off for Holmes Hole.

April 5, 1779, Nonamessett Island

...This morning, Monday 5th, one armed vessel proceeded to Nonnamesit Island, and sent off a boat to get the provisions they had killed and left there; but a party of our people got there before them, and prevented their landing, and some boats of ours had like to have cut them off from the sloop. Upon the boat's getting to the sloop, they hasted to join the fleet which then made sail, as they said, for Nantucket.

A boat landed at Martha's Vineyard, where they shot a few cattle, sheep, and hogs, which they carried off, paying for two sheep only. They told the Vineyard people they had sent one sloop to Rhode Island, with cowards who had refused to fight, but probably the wounded. The party consisted of Tories. Some of them were known to have gone from this State. The commander was said to be one Winslow; the second in command one Leonard. (f.II-456-458)

Falmouth Militia Repels Loyalist Invasion. Franklin L. Gifford, 1930s.

The Town of Sherburne in the Island of Nantucket.

10
Nantucket Raided

April 5, 1779, Nantucket

Extract from Starbuck, *The History of Nantucket* **(1924)**

Early in April seven small vessels made their appearance, coming from the westward. Five of them anchored off the bar and two entered the harbor and made fast at the wharf. They proved to be manned by Refugees and to have been sent by the Commander in Chief at New York to ascertain the disposition or the people, whether their sympathies were with King George or the Continental Congress. They were under orders not to molest the "peaceable" inhabitants, those who were friendly to the Crown, but to destroy Rebel property wherever it could be found. Eldad Tupper, a somewhat notorious Royalist was with them. As the Refugees were almost wholly people who had practically been ostracized by the patriots and much of their property confiscated, they were by no means reluctant about the carrying out of their orders. (s.210)

Extract from Freeman,
History of Cape Cod, Annals of Falmouth **(1862)**

...They landed [at Nantucket], near 200-strong, entered the town with drawn swords and fixed bayonets, and styled themselves "Loyal Refugees," professing to act under commission from the commander-in-chief of the Br. forces at Newport. They owned that they had been to Falmouth and Intended to have landed; but the rebels, who lay in ambush, fired upon them, killing 15 and wounding 20, who were sent in a sloop to Rhode Island; that Edward Winslow, formerly of Plymouth, was commanding officer when at Falmouth, was wounded; and gone to Newport with a ball in his breast. This was told by the sentries, though George Leonard, formerly of Boston, pretended that it was gout,—this Leonard being next in command, and Pelham Winslow, formerly of Plymouth, next to him. One Murray, of Rutland, stood next. There were with them two of Brig. Ruggles's sons.... They said they should come again, very soon and chastise any who should abuse those who were friendly to them. Doctor ---- [Gelston?] was very busy with them, and they showed great partiality for their brother Tories. From the above, compared with what they confessed at Nonnameset and the Vineyard, we have reason to think Col. Freeman and the brave men under his command gave the poor rascals a decent drubbing.

...In their invasion of Nantucket, they made proclamation that they were "come for the property of the rebellious subjects of America," mentioning particularly Thos. Jenkins and Timo. Fitch. In plundering, the first store they broke into was that of Jenkins, which they cleared of a great quantity of goods, 200 bls. of oil, 2,000 lbs. of whalebone, and stripped it of everything, even to some chalk and an old grindstone. They broke open a number of other stores, and took large quantities of oil, molasses, sugar. coffee, and all kinds of goods that fell in their way, 30 or 40 suits of sails with anchors, cables, tow-lines, great quantities of cordage, rigging, etc., also the whole craft and provisions they came across. A hundred and fifty men or more were employed from 4 P.M. on Monday, to 6 next morning in plundering, insulting, and abusing the inhabitants,—compelling them to truck down to the vessels whatever they had taken from them.

They at last were told that a 20-gun ship and a privateer were coming to take them. They retreated precipitately, carrying with them most of their plunder, leaving some loaded carts which they dare not delay for. They carried off two brigs with cargoes bound to the West Indies, 2 or 3 schooners, and a large number of boats. Some things they could not carry off they destroyed. (f.II-459)

Deborah Chase
A Young Quaker Lady of Nantucket

On one of these forays of the Refugees, it is related that their sentinels were so posted that it was difficult for the people to procure water. Among those who suffered were Deborah Chase and her parents. Deborah's patience finally was exhausted and she determined to procure the water at all hazards. Her father remonstrated in vain, telling her: "Thee had better not; thee will get a bayonet in thee!" She replied that she "would as lief die one way as another," and seizing two pails she started. In passing a corner a sergeant on guard, presented his bayonet to stop her. Without delay she hurled a pail full in his face knocking him senseless on the ground, bleeding profusely. She passed on, filled her pails with water, and returned in safety past the still prostrate sentry.

Miss Chase was a young woman who was not to be trifled with. There was at one time try-works located near the head of the New North wharf where the vessels as they brought in black fish left them to be tryed out. The oil when extracted was drawn off into large, shallow pans to cool. At one time after their work, the men wanted some bread and sent to the bake house of her parents nearby for a supply. The little girl who usually carried it was too small, so Deborah volunteered to go with it. Among the men was one who had just been married and was wearing his bridal coat. When he saw Deborah coming he announced his intention to kiss her. She recommended him not to try, but he persisted and seized hold of her. She caught him at a disadvantage and whirling him suddenly landed him in the middle of the pan of cooling oil.

On another occasion a man driving past her house in a cart drove unnecessarily close. She admonished him to be more careful. In a spirit of bravado he repeated the offence; whereupon, she rushed out and seizing hold of his cart overturned it in the street. (s.210)

April 12, 1779, Newport

George Leonard to Mr. Joseph Talor

The narrative of our late expedition transmitted to our agents, will informe of the Success we met with, at the Island of Nantucket. The Captures made at that place, you will please to Libel in the Names, of the following armed Vessels: the Sloop *General Lesslie*, Capt. DOW, Schooner *Experiment*, Capt. MacPHERSON; Sloop *Times*, Capt. McCLEAN, Sloop *General Mathew*, Capt. FORSYTH, Schooner *Sally*, Capt. SPELLING; the Sloop *Harriot* Tender to the *General Lesslie* all which were employed on this expedition.

Their may disputes arrise, with the Capts. of the privateer wether the *Genl. Lesslie* is intitled to Share with the Rest of the armed vessels; as it was not present at the time of the Seizures. The Above mentioned vessels Sailed in Concert from the harbour of Newport, all to be Jointly Concerned, after reaching Falmouth, the time had expired for the Return of Capt. DePEYSTERr's Company of granadears; Col. WINSLOW the Commanding Officer of the troops, Demanded of me, a Convoy for that Company to Rhode Island. The *Genl. Lesslie* was ordered for that purpose; her being a Safe Vessel & most formidable: with Col. WINSLOW on board seized with a Violent fit of the gout in the stomach, and not able to be removed—upon her departure she was ordered to return to the fleet, which was done emmediately, but previous to her Return, the Captures were made, She joined us at homes hole, in the Vineyard Sound where we was all glad to met her, as a further security to our prise Vessels—

As a Commanding Officer of the armed Vessels, I removed from the *Experiment*, on board the *Lesslie* and took the prises under her Convoy, to Rhode Island the Signals from that time, were given from her, untill the whole fleet arrived safe into this harbour—these are the Circumstances you will therefore take proper Steps to Libel the Captures in her name, with the Rest of the Armed Vessels—The Refugees to a man employed on this expedition, have agreed to Support this Claim;

The *General Prescott* is preparing to take in her guns, with her, and the rest of our Small fleet, I hope to give a Sufficient Convoy to the Refugees on these present excursions and Sone to Sail in Vessel, the *Lesslie*, with the *George* is to make a Short Course, untill we get ready for another expedition—

Of all this you will acquaint Mr. BLACK, and give my Compliment to him—

I am Yours Sincerely,

Geo. LEONARD

P.S: I am Sorrey it is not in my power, to give you a exact Return, of the articles taken; they Consist of oil—Whale—Cordage—molasses—Sugar—paints—tobagoe—fish—Board—Iron—Steel &c &c &c on Board two Briggs & a Schooner; which you will Libel, there names unknown—Many articles were brought from thence in the *General Prescott* with two other transport Sloops one of which, the General Lent me, the other I chartered; one of the Briggs is a remarkable Sailer; if She is Sold at a moderate price, I shall incline to purchase her—

I here enclose you an imperfect Invoice, you will Judge what Artecles to get Condemned with the Vessels; you will Lose no time, for the Condemnation on the Vessels, & Effects, which may prevent Disputes with the privateerman. (o.)

April 12, 1779, Nantucket

Extract from the Memoranda of William Rotch
From Starbuck, *The History of Nantucket* (1924)

We soon had information that Leonard & Co. were preparing another and more formidable expedition to visit us. The Town was convened to consult what measures should be taken in this trying emergency [April 9 and April 12, 1779], which resulted in sending Dr. Benjamin Tupper, Samuel Starbuck and myself [William Roach] to New Port and thence, if necessary, to New York to represent our case to the Commanders of the Navy and Army.

We arrived in the Harbor of New Port, where Capt. Dawson commanded the Navy, and Gen. Prescott the Army. But the American Refugees had made interest with the Gen. not to suffer us to land, and we were ordered by Dawson to depart. We interceded with him to let us stay a little longer, for we found the expedition was progressing rapidly, and unless we could arrest it, it would be in vain to proceed to New York. Dawson by request of Gen. Prescott, under the influence of the Refugees, ordered our immediate departure again. Dr. Tupper now, for the first time, went on board, and in his plain, blunt way, after the usual ceremony of entry, addressed him in this manner: "You order us to depart. We cannot be frightened, nor, will we depart. We know the extent of your authority. You may make a prize of our vessel, and imprison us; much better for us to be thus treated than to be sent away. We came here for peace, and you ought to encourage everything of this kind" &c.

His reasons made such an impression upon Captain Dawson that he gave us liberty to stay as long as we pleased. The Refugee boat came several times to us, to get us off. We insisted on going on shore, but they as often refused us. After this conversation with Dawson, the boat came again, and Dr. Tupper insisted that he would go on shore. They still denied him unless he intended to stay with them. As he was not always exact in his expressions, to answer his purpose, he says: "Well, I am going to stay," and almost forcibly got into their boat and went on shore, being satisfied that if he could once see the Gen. he could, in this respect, destroy the influence of the Refugees.

He accordingly got liberty for Samuel Starbuck to come on shore and the next day for me to follow. We found it necessary to be in friendship with the Refugees, that, if possible, we might stop the current of their intended predatory visit. I got on shore in the afternoon, and found that I must wait on Gen. Prescott. Knowing his brittle temper, and it being in the afternoon I almost dreaded to appear in his presence. However, let my treatment be what it would, I wished it over, and accordingly went.

I was introduced to him by one of his aids. He received me very cordially, gave me his hand, and said: "Mr. Rotch, will you have some dinner? I can give you good bread, though the Rebels say we have none." I thanked him, saying I had dined. "Well, will you take a glass of wine?" I answered, I have no objection if thou canst put up with my plain way. The glass was filled with his own, and those of all the officers at table, and as a stranger introduced, they all drank to me before I put the glass to my lips. I then observed to the Gen., "As I mentioned before, if thou couldst put up with my plain way, I was willing to take wine with thee, but as we as a society disuse these ceremonies, I have always found it best to keep to my profession, let me be in what company I may. Therefore I hope my not making a like return will not be accepted as any mark of disrespect, for I assure you that it is not the case." His answer was "Oh, no, if a Quaker will but be a Quaker, it is all I want of him. But --- --- is no Quaker" (mentioning one of our profession), and I wos sorry for the cause of his remarks. (s.211)

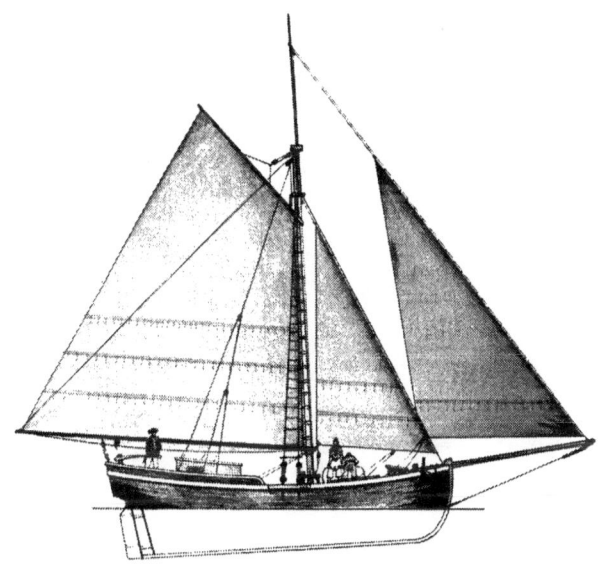

Colonial Trading Sloop.

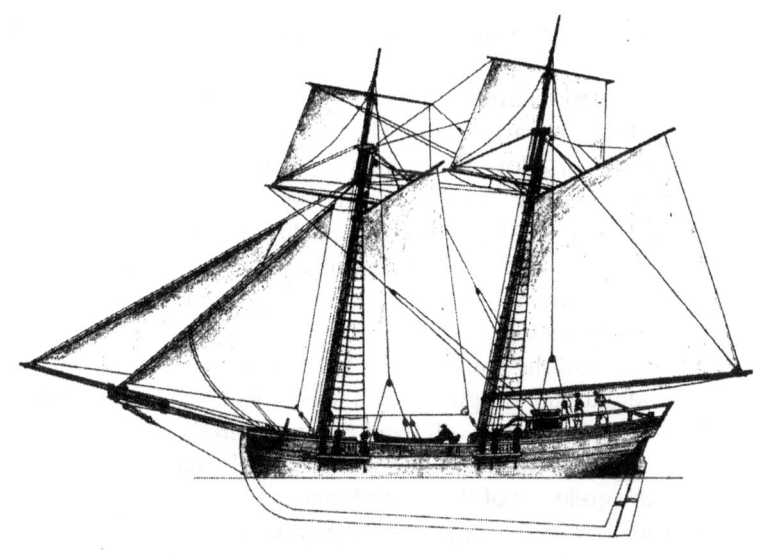

Colonial Schooner.

11

Joseph Dimmick

May 1779, Tarpaulin Cove

Extract from Freeman,
History of Cape Cod, Annals of Falmouth **(1862)**

A schooner sent to Connecticut River for corn [for Woods Hole], then extremely scarce in these parts and selling at $3.00 per bushel, was intercepted on her return, just as she was entering the Sound. The Captain of the craft escaped to the shore in his boat, distressed by the loss of his vessel and cargo; and hastened from Woods Hole to Col. Dimmick, whom he reached at midnight, the distance being about 7 miles and to whom he communicated the facts. Col. Dimmick jumped at once from his bed, whilst dressing gave the captain encouraging words, and directed him for economy of time, to go at once to the residence of his brother Lot and arouse him. The Colonel and Mr. Lot Dimmick soon succeeded in mustering 20 resolute men, and started for Woods Hole.

They there procured three whale boats, and proceeded silently to Tarpaulin Cove, arriving just before day break. It was very cold and the Colonel allowed his men to land and kindle a fire in a hollow, where they would be unobserved, and there wait for morning. At the first glimmering of day, the privateer with his prize was discovered lying at anchor in the Cove. Col. Dimmick and men were, another moment, in their boats pulling silently but vigorously for the prize. They were fired on from both vessels, but quickly returned the compliment, boarded the prize, retook it, got immediately under weigh and ran it ashore at the West end of the Vineyard. The privateer followed and was repulsed, the tide rose, and in a few hours the schooner was safely moored at Woods Hole, to the great joy of the inhabitants.

Dimmick was courage-inspiring, prompt in all emergencies, and always found brave men who were ready at his lead. (f.II-470)

May 1779, Nantucket

Extract from Starbuck, *The History of Nantucket* (1924)

There seems to be an entire harmony of opinion among the predatory chiefs, whether it was Leonard of the Refugees or Dimmick of the Continentals, and the point on which they agreed was that Nantucket was a fine field in which to work.

In May, 1779, Major Dimmick made a return of sundry goods "taken by Men in Arms...From the Island of Nantucket," the operation being performed under his personal direction. The list included chairs, tables, hand-irons, large lever, trunks, book case, low chest of drawers, small box, bedsteads, old rug, high chest of draws, several casks of oil etc., etc. Christopher Hussey Jr., and Daniel Starbuck, in whose custody the articles were, made affidavits as to the ownership of the goods. It is difficult from any present view point to see of what use the majority of the articles taken could be to the captors. (s.230)

**Extract From Rago,
"Alarm at Falmouth 1779"**

Falmouth was never an epicenter of privateering like Bedford, Marblehead or Providence, but at least five privateers operated out of Falmouth: the *Defence*, a six-gun [swivels], fifteen-man boat commanded by Silas Hatch, Jr.; the *Falmouth*, a seven-gun, thirty-man boat commanded by Barakiah Bassett; the *Seaflower*, a four-gun, forty man sloop commanded by Robinson Jones; the four-gun, thirty-man sloop *Union*, commanded by Lot Dimmick. Moreover, the town operated dozens of smaller whaleboats when specific situations arose. (r.12)

**Joseph Dimmick
Extract from Freeman,
History of Cape Cod, Annals of Falmouth (1862)**

Gen. JOSEPH DIMMICK was early in his country's service. He had been a lieutenant of militia under Gen. Abercrombie, at Ticonderoga. At the commencement of the Revolution, he at once took a bold and decided stand. The cause of liberty and independence was espoused by him in faith and zeal with unflinching firmness and determination. He represented this town in the general court of 1779; in 1788 was appointed high sheriff, which office he held 20 years; was elected to the senate in 1808, and continued three years; and in 1808, was appointed justice of the peace et quorum, and also of the court of sessions.

Every trust reposed in him he executed with dignity, fidelity, and honor. He was, withal, a consistent Christian. On public religious services, he was a constant attendant; and in the domestic circle, the uniformly-devout worshipper. As a public man, or private citizen, he was public-spirited, humane, generous, always courteous and kind; his affectionate disposition was ever marked by unusual fondness for, and attentions to, little children, who seldom passed by him in the street, without a kindly recognition, and in return were always proud of having "made their manners to Gen. Dimmick."

We well remember this trait; for his intimacy with our honored parent gave us frequent opportunities, when a child, of seeing him under the parental roof and under his, own. His personal appearance was that of one of Nature's noblemen; his heavy and shaggy brow, finely-chiseled features, his noble form, all bespeaking for him a combination of true greatness and excellence. As a PATRIOT, he stood conspicuous; and yet so modest and unassuming that the respect shown him seemed to be regarded by him as unmerited kindness.

When in Boston at a certain time, on business and receiving a formal and very unexpected invitation from Gov. Hancock to dine, he was amazed to find so large a party of eminent men and notable ladies assembled, and, on entering the dining-hall, was still more astonished, when particularly assigned by Gov. H, to the seat of honor at the table. His daring exploits are generally and chiefly dwelt upon; but his honest patriotism, his uniform integrity, his symmetry of character, are, after all, his crowning glory. (f.II-470)

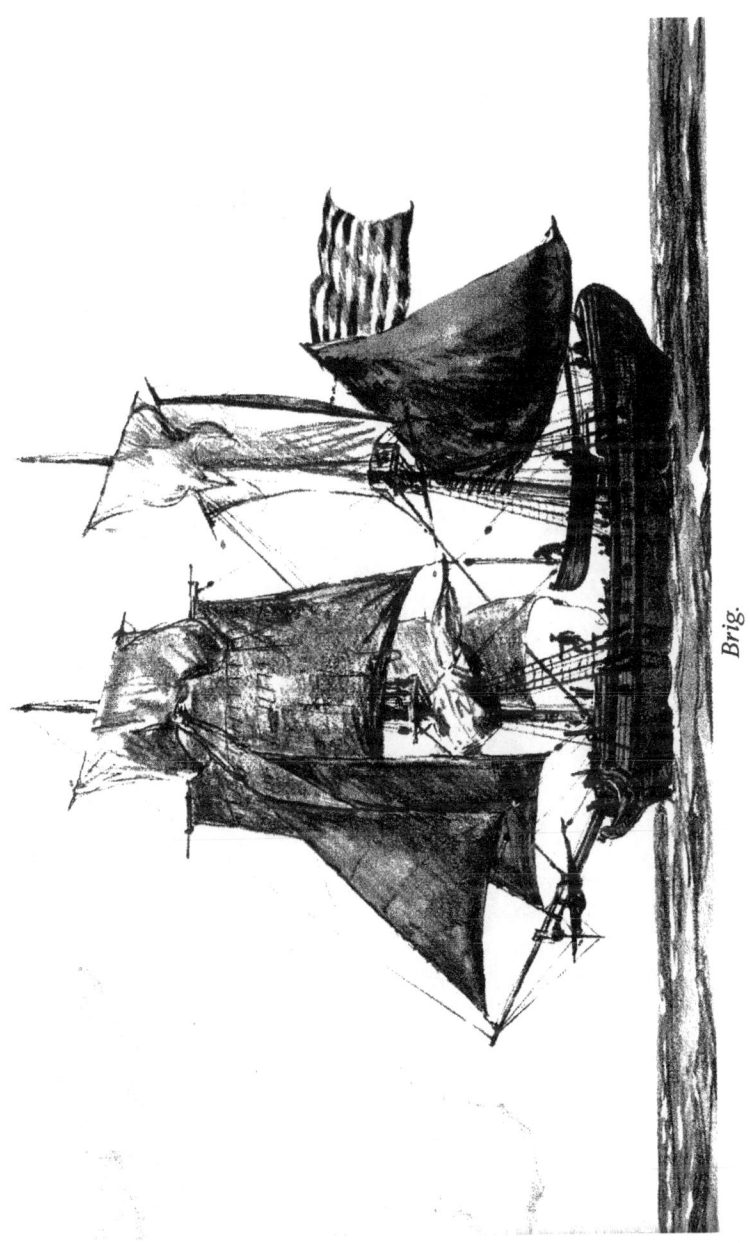

Brig.

Sulky Captured by the Privateer Washington, Entering Newberryport under a Prize Crew, January 15, 1776.

12
The Refugee Fleet Returns

General Return of Vessels, Stock & other Articles taken from the Rebels by the Associated Refugees & other Loyalists between the Comencement of the Association & the 10th June 1779.

Date	Place	Items
February 1779	Narriganset [?]	Sloop, 19 Oxen & Cows, 166 Sheep.
February 1779	Prudence	102 Horses.
April 6th 1779	Nantucket	2 Brigantines, 2 Schooners, 8 Boats.
April 26th 1779	Noman's Land	2 Oxen & Cows, 580 Sheep, 200 Lambs.
May 8th 1779	Point Judith	2 Boats, 53 Oxen & Cows, 1000 Sheep, 400 Lambs, 15 Calves.

May 19th 1779	Narishawn	32 Horses.
May 21st 1779	Quidnecit	29 Oxen & Cows, 17 Sheep, 11 Hogs, 6 Lambs, 8 Calves.
June 6th 1779	South Kingston	35 Oxen & Cows, 80 Sheep, 36 Lambs, 15 Calves.

Total- 2 Brigantines, 2 Schooners, 1 Sloop, 10 Boats, 134 Horses, 138 Oxen & Cows, 1843 Sheep, 11 Hogs, 642 Lambs, 38 Calves.

Sundries- 1 Cargoe Tobacco & Lumber and 1 Cargoe Lumber on board Brigs, 16 vessels sails, 180 Casks oyl, 12 Cass. Whale Bone, 3 tons Barr iron, 3 tons Cordage, 15 Hhds molasses, 2 bbls sugar, 1 Cask refind. Spermalaste [?], 15 Bbls Beef, 1 Cask Pearl Ash, & variety of small articles. 42 stands of Small-Arms with Bayonets & Cartouch Boxes. Prisoners at different times 35 among whom are some persons of considerable Note.

Ed. WINSLOW Lt. Coll: Comdt. Refugees (o.)

July 7, 1779, Sherbourne [Nantucket Village]

**Report of the Committee to the
Inhabitants of the Town of Sherbourne
Extract from Starbuck,** *The History of Nantucket* **(1924)**

Agreeably to your appointment, we proceeded to Newport and New York, and presented the memorial to the Commander-in-chief of the British army and navy, and after repeated applications, we received their answers (Sir Henry Clinton's was only verbal), assuring us, that he had given orders that no further depredation should be made upon the island, on property belonging to the inhabitants, by persons under the authority of Great Britain; Sir George Collier gave us the same assurance in writing; and for a full knowledge of his disposition, we refer you to the enclosed declaration...

...By Sir George Collier, Commodore and Commander-in-Chief of His Majesty's ships and vessels employed in North America, from the North Cape on the Island of Cape Breton, to the Bahama Islands and Florida, inclusive; As great numbers of the inhabitants of the island of Nantucket are represented to me to be of the sect called Quakers, and consequently not accustomed to bear arms, and believing the remainder of the inhabitants to be quiet, inoffensive people, who have already suffered severely the calamities of war, I therefore think proper to forbid all privateers, letters of marque armed vessels, or bodies of armed men, from molesting, ravaging or plundering, the estates, houses, or persons, of the inhabitants of the said island; and if any shall be found to act inconsistently with these directions, their commissions as privateers, or letters of marque, shall be, vacated, and themselves punished for the offence. Given on board His Majesty's Ship, the Raisonable, off New York, 23d June, 1779 (Signed) George Collier. By command of the Commander, John Marr Sec'y. (s.218)

July 19, 1779, New York

Recruiting Poster
The New York Gazette and the Weekly Mercury

THE FRIGATE *RESTORATION*
(Formerly the *OLIVER CROMWELL*),
is now fitting for sea, and will be ready in six days to join the
ASSOCIATED REFUGEE FLEET,
Lying in Huntington Harbour, and intending soon to pay a visit to the Rebel Coast:
ALL GENTLEMEN who are desirous to enter on board said ship as officers, shall be provided for agreeable to their merit; and all good SEAMEN who wish to join this determined band of LOYALISTS, are desired to repair on board said ship, lying at the Navy-Yard, where they shall receive
FIVE GUINEAS, Advance,
THREE POUNDS, Sterling

Per month, and one share of all property taken from his Majesty's revolted subjects by sea and land.

Mr. LEONARD flatters himself, that this encouragement will be sufficient to induce every well wisher to his Majesty and the British Constitution, to engage in an undertaking, where profit and honor are inseparably blended.

N.B. As Mr. LEONARD is determined, at all events, to adhere punctiliously to the orders of the Commander in Chief both by sea and land, he warns all persons who are engaged in either service not to apply, unless with permission, for he must and will reject them. (o.)

September 7, 1779, Newport

George Leonard to Mr. [Joseph] TAYLOR

Dear TAYLOR

The few minutes I had at Huntington would not permit me to write from thence, as the wind was fair, and I was unwilling to lose so favorable an opportunity. The 31st of August we arriv'd in this harbour with a fleet of 38 Sail; my time since has been constantly employed in settling all my accounts; I have paid all the seamen belonging to the several vessels both their prize money and wages to their entire satisfaction, excepting Captain DOW, whom nothing short of the nett proceeds of the vessel and the money due to the poor seamen, would prevent grumbling. Within this hour he has been ordered before the Superintendant to answer for his conduct in plundering the defenceless family on Gardiners island; I hope the provost will be his fate, as no inconvenience will arise to the concern'd in consequence of it.

Our little fleet which consists of nine Sail has been ready to depart ever since the 5th instant with every thing necessary to execute our intended plan, the wind only prevents. I have taken on board the Brig and Schooner a variety of articles for the market at Nantucket and Martha's Vineyard, also cash with me for purchasing oyl, candles &c &c if no misfortune happens, you may expect the Brig soon at N. York. Doctor TUPPER, who was lately from thence informs me there is one or two valuable cargoes, ready to be brought off. Mr. GOLDSBOROUGH will be more particular respecting Dr. TUPPER.

I have enter'd into a solemn contract with the refugees, to have an exclusive right to all the trade with those islands; they are to have on their part the nett proceeds of the Cattle, Sheep and Poultry on Marthas Vineyard only, after paying charges of collecting & transporting, and 5 P Cent to a factor, whom I shall appoint to do the business.

Thus much has been done in the short interval I have been here, we are all in the highest spirits and full expectations of compleating the wood and other contracts. I have engaged Mr. Elisha JONES to cut and cart to low water mark at Eatons neck one thousand Chords of firewood. On the delivery I am to pay him three dollars and three quarters, per chord. Be kind enough to send some person to see this contract performed. Mr. DORNETT, will enclose this together with all other papers necessary for you to see.

I have not offer'd the subscriptions here; the favors I have receiv'd from General PRESCOT, Capt. SAVAGE and others lately, make it a matter of delicacy with me. If we succeed agreeable to our sanguine expectations I hope there will be no necessity to ask assistance of the traders here, who will think, the whole refugee fleet always at their service, and demand a privilidge of trading to the islands, should they contribute.

My best respects to Mr. JEFFERS & Mr. ROYE, I feel a grateful sense of Mr. JEFFERS friendship, while at New York. Mr. DORNETT will forward from Genl. PRESCOTT a permit for Shipping two hundred puncheons Rum.

I am Your Sincere & obedt. Servt.

Geo. LEONARD (o.)

September 9, 1779, Newport
Major Joshua Upham to Mr. Taylor

The *Restoration* sail'd on ye 8th from hence for the Vineyard.

He [Mr. LEONARD] proposed going to Old Town, has carried with him what Goods he pleased. The Genl. is disposed to afford him every assistance. What will be the Event is very uncertain, whether Wood can be had in that Quarter must depend on the good or ill Disposition of the Inhabitants. I think it is very clear that much Stock, by which I mean in the stile of a Darmer, much Cattle Sheep &c may be obtained in Exchange for Goods & that many Goods in that Way may be disposed of, this being the Policy adopted by the General.

Two Refugees viz. a Mr. BANKER & Mr. THAXTER came in last Evening by the Way of Nantucket. They inform us of the Destruction of the rebel Fleet at the Eastward excepting two Vessels captured by Sir George viz. the Brig *Hunter* of 20 Guns & a Ship, the first with the *Galatea* are cruising from Cape Cod & Capan. The Frigates at Boston are not manned on which Account cannot come out as yet.

These Men called, on their Way hither, at the Elizabeth Islands w[h]ere they found that the Rebels had got Intelligence that our Armament was intended, against Bedford, Falmouth & these Islands. That the Rebels were collecting at the two first Places for the Purpose of defending. That the Cattle &c on the Elizabeth Islands were taken & taking away by the Rebels. That the Rebels had been informed of our Intention of getting Wood at Naushon. I think this Conduct of the Rebels in taking away Cattle &c will induce the Inhabitants of the Vineyard, from whence the Cattle are not removed, to dispose of their Cattle &c to us for Goods or Hard Money rather than to them for Paper Money, the Exchange of which is 20 for one. I think nothing is to be feared from the rebel Navy at present, I therefore hope that something will be effected to your Advantage.

Mr. LEONARD has contracted for the cutting &c of 1000 Cord of Wood at Eatons Neck, near Lloyds Neck. I wish it had been for two instead of one Thousand Cord.

I intend in few Days to go to our Friends at Old-Town, should have gone with them but the General was displeased at my Absence when last I left the Garrison & would not hear of my going again at present. Shall get his leave to go down, I doubt not, in a few Days on a Visit.

I hope something will be done by the Cruising of some of the armed Vessels at Nantucket & at & near Nomans Lands. In Short, the undertaking is great & the Event must at present remain very uncertain, but, my good Friend, you need not be told that my every Exertion shall be added to those of the Party.

Expect in a few Days to hear from them & from that Information we shall be inabled to form a Judgment with some Degree of Certainty of your future Success.

Am sorry to be informed that our Friend BLOWERS is prevented coming to this Place by his sickness & that of his sister. Am sure he will come by the first Opportunity.

The Business of supplying Goods will, if the Post be maintained for any Length of Time, be very considerable. Of this you will be better informed by the next Opportunity. If you wish to communicate any thing to me on the subject I am sure you will do it with freedom & that you will command me in this & every other Matter where it is possible for me to serve you.

I am sincerely your Friend &c.

[Major] Joshua UPHAM (o.)

September 12, 1779, Newport

Thomas A. Coffin, an Officer in the British Army, to Colonel Fanning
Newport, Rhode Island, 25 September, 1779

...Before I proceed farther in my journal of occurrences, I shall beg leave to observe that the Inhabitants of the Elizabeth Islands are now in a predicament peculiar to themselves. Their situation is such as to admit of a free and constant intercourse with the people of the Main, while their interviews with those in the Kings service are accidental, seldom and short. Reports favorable to the Rebels are circulated with extreme assiduity; prejudices are imbibed, and for want of authentic intelligence, egregious mistakes are made relative to important facts.

At the commencement of hostilities, they engaged with reluctance, because they were exceedingly exposed to depredation from either party; but at length, by the stratagems of the Rebels & their immediate influence from local circumstances, they were seduced into the commissions of open acts of treason, and they continued in arms against the King until they were deprived of them by Maj. Gen. Grey in Sept. 1778. He also obliged them to furnish considerable supplies for the Kings' Garrisons. By this exertion of the British troops they were not only more confirmed in their ideas of danger, but they were also furnished with a sufficient apology for remaining in a state of neutrality and peace.

The Rebels (altho averse to relinquishment of their commission over them) did not suppose them of such consequence as to risk an army in their defence, but left them to make the best terms they could obtain on all occasions, still exercising a right of taxation, and obliging them to pay respect and obedience to the laws enacted by their usurped powers.... (e.299)

September 13, 1779, Nantucket

Extract from Starbuck, *The History of Nantucket* (1924)

...About the middle of September three English privateers entered the harbor. While there a small American privateer sloop anchored inside the bar near the Cliffs. The Refugees who were with the English privateers, carried a cannon to the Cliffs and fired several shot at the American vessel but to no effect, for at high tide the American weighed anchor and went over the bar again. The failure of the Refugees to capture or disable the American privateer was evidently a matter of considerable annoyance for on September 14 the day following the bombardment from the Cliffs, Messers Tupper, Rotch and Starbuck were summoned by Leonard, Refugee Commander, to meet him at Martha's Vineyard. Among other things the Islanders were accused of was having assisted the American privateer to escape.

Upon the return of the committee on September 18, a Town meeting was immediately convened to consider the demands of the Refugees. It was voted that the Town disavowed any hostile proceedings against the English or had done anything to forfeit the favors received. It was also voted to present the British forces with an ox to replace the "one that they had lost."

Timothy Folger, Stephen Paddack and Dr. Gelston were appointed a committee to draw up a memorial and present it to the English commanders. (s.218)

September 18, 1779, Falmouth

The Examination of John Lorrance

The examination of John Lorrance and four negroes, deserters from the fleet in Vineyard Sound taken at Falmouth the 18th. day of September 1779: The fleet consists of 10 sail of vessell in all and 259 men designed to ye Vineyard for wood, with written orders to distress ye inhabitants on ye main by burning or making depredations in any other way they see fit. The account of each vessell they gave as follows, viz:

Type	Name	Guns	Men	Remarks
Ship	Restoration	20	120	
Sloop	Preston	12	25	
Sloop	Garth	8	12	From which they deserted
Sloop	Green	10	12	
Sloop	Leslie	10	16	
Schooner	Charlotte	12	23	
Schooner	(small)	2	8	& 10 swivels
Schooner	(small)	0	3	& 2 swivels
Schooner		0	6	Saml. Perry Commander formerly of Sandwich
Schooner		0	4	

Attested before Joseph Dimick Falmouth the 18th. day of September 1779. (e.298)

Late September 1779, Nantucket Sound

Gen. Joseph Otis to Daniel Davis, Esq.
Extract from Freeman,
History of Cape Cod, Annals of Barnstable **(1858)**

"Yesterday the *Tories* in the Sound, about a league off Highano's [Hyannis] harbor, took a vessel bound out of said harbor to Stonington, owned by one Palmer, loaded with dry fish; and drove another ashore on the eastward part of Falmouth, loaded with cheese, cider, &c. They cut the vessel's deck to pieces, as the owners had scuttled her. In short, the refugees have got a number of Vineyard pilot-boats (about 20) and man them, and run into our shores and take every thing that floats." Gen. Otis applies for "eight-pounders, swivels," &c.; and engages "to procure two small vessels and get them manned to scour the sound." He says, "Highanos is much exposed; and to draw off the men to Falmouth causes much uneasiness." (f.I-525)

Late September 1779, Old Town [Edgartown] Harbor

Extract from Freeman,
History of Cape Cod, Annals of Falmouth **(1862)**

...a messenger arrived at Col. Dimmick's, in the evening, giving information that two British privateers were at Old Town Harbor with a prize-schooner just taken. The col., in a few minutes, mustered 25 men, proceeded with them to Woods Hole, procured a sloop, and sailed for Edgartown, Capt. Thomas Jones acting as pilot. Leaving Woods Hole at 2 o'clock, they reached Old Town Harbor at the first dawning of day, and saw, to their surprise, that a British ship-of-war was in Holmes Hole Harbor. Determined, however, not to be foiled, although they saw they could not weather the outward privateer, they ran past her while she was in the act of firing signals for the ship to come to her relief; boarded and carried the innermost privateer, though manned by 33 men, and, in a few moments, although cut off from a retreat in the direction of Woods Hole, or any part of Falmouth, put the vessels before the wind and ran for Oyster Island, in Barnstable, where they arrived safe with their prize, landed their 33 manacled prisoners, and sent them off to Boston by land as prisoners of war. (f.II-470)

October 12, 1779, Falmouth

Extract from Freeman,
History of Cape Cod, Annals of Barnstable **(1858)**

...despatches from Gen. Otis show that "George Leonard has sent a flag of truce for exchange of prisoners." He represents Leonard as at the head of "a refugee gang in the sound." Leonard was desirous of exchanging "Barnabas Eldridge and Isaac Matthews of

Yarmouth held as prisoners, and Manasses Swift and James Wing of Falmouth on parole," for certain "men taken by Falmouth people" at the capture of "the *Gen. Leslie* in Old Town harbor."
  Gen. Otis says, "The taking of the *Gen. Leslie* was a bold and gallant action. She had twenty-seven men and ten four-pounders; the Falmouth vessel had twenty-five men, and two three-pounders, with two *wooden guns*. They went to Old Town harbor where lay the *Leslie* and a sloop mounting twelve nine-pounders, with three prizes anchored between them. They first made for the twelve-gun sloop, intending to board her and sweep the harbor; but, the wind and tide setting out, fell about a biscuit toss astern, and could not fetch again. This was night work. The sloop being alarmed, began to fire. They then immediately run the *Leslie* aboard amidst the fire from the other sloop—firing a volley of small arms into the *Leslie*, wounding one of her men since dead, and receiving a volley which hurt nobody; then jumping on board, about twenty men drove the *Leslie's* men below, cut the cable, and brought the *Leslie* to Highanos [Hyannis]." "Capt. Dimmick of Falmouth" is mentioned as the hero of this transaction. (f.I-527)

October 20, 1779, Newport

George Leonard to Coll. NORTON, Wm. JENNIGAN Esqr. & Capt. John PEAS, Martha's Vineyard

Gentlemen:
  On my arrival at Rhode Island I received orders to hold myself in readiness with the rest of the fleet, and proceed to New York. It is not probable I shall be at the Vineyard this winter, You will therefore take such measures, as may be thought proper, to forward me the accounts of the Cattle, Sheep, Poultry &c purchased and not paid for—also the quantity of wood brought off—nothing shall be wanting on my part that Justice is done to the inhabitants of Martha's Vineyard.
  I am your Friend & humb. Servt.
                                                            Geo. LEONARD (o)

Widow's Walk.

13
Nantucket's Protracted Suffering

Extracts from Starbuck, *The History of Nantucket* (1924)

...Some time in the year 1780, Admiral Arbuthnot returned to England, and Admiral Digby succeeded him. As soon as Arbuthnot was gone, those plundering Refugees were upon us again, our protection having ceased by his departure. This renewed our perplexity...Nantucket seemed to be a focusing point for small detachments of Refugees and Colonials, and quite a large number of encounters of those minor hostile forces occurred on and in the immediate vicinity of the Island. Indeed the isolated and defenceless condition of Nantucket seemed to invite just such forays. It was very difficult at times to keep many of the people from expressing a justifiable indignation and actively imposing the insolence and thievery of the Refugees, and openly attacking the crews of small English privateers as well as the bands of predatory traitors to their country, who were as much worse than the more manly British armed forces, as the cowardly sneak thief is worse than the open highwayman. In not a few instances, even members of the Society of Friends seemed to have allowed their indignation, or instinct of self-preservation, to overcome their religious scruples.

...In all probability Capt. Dimmick was of material assistance to the Nantucket People in Repelling Refugee forays. (s.239)

July 8, 1781, Nantucket

Early in July, 1781, the Refugees renewed their depredations upon the people of Nantucket. On the 8th of that month, two shaving mills from New York came into the harbor to secure provisions. They captured several small vessels and chased others into the harbor. On the 9th Major Dimmick of Falmouth, and a crew, came to the Island in pursuit of the enemy. The combatant had a brief engagement in which one man was killed and two severely wounded, but without any decisive result. The Refugees captured a schooner belonging to William Barnard and sent it to New York, allowing the captain and crew to go ashore. (s.238)

September 29, 1781, Nantucket

On September 29, there was a large party of nearly 100 Refugees entered the harbor for the purpose of plundering the people. Major Dimmick again engaged them and succeeded in driving them away, but evidently did not feel that his force, which was only about two thirds as large as that of the Refugees, was strong enough to pursue them. (s.238)

March 25, 1782, Nantucket

Among the instances showing the annoyance and abuse to which the Islanders were subjected may be noted the following as recorded by Mrs. Fanning in her Diaries:

Several Refugees in the sound—have taken Riddle coming from Connecticut with provisions, & Crosby also—Ben Russel came in today & brought the news—they chased him but he escaped...

March 21, 1782

...William Rotch & some women were bound off to meeting yesterday & were taken by a shaving mill carried under Gay Head & anchored—Dimick went over from Falmouth just before the squall yesterday & took the mill, retook Rotch—the shavers robb'd the women's pockets, took out their Buckels & abused them much.

March 31, 1782

...Reuben Macy was lately taken with 3000 Bushels of Salt on Board & carried into N. York.

April 5, 1782

...Peleg Eason came to the Bar yesterday from Turk's Island with a Load of Salt (was gone from here 6 weeks to a day) soon after he came to the Bar a Privateer schooner out of New York came to the

Barr took the Brigg into Possession. Wm Rotch jun'r & Sam'll Rodman (owners of the Brigg) went on Board, Ransom'd her for a very small consideration. This morn the Brigg came into the harbour. The Privateer has taken this forenoon a schooner from Boston belonging to John Beane loaded with Lumber; (he purchased the Vessel there in Boston & her Load). Several people have been off to try to get the Vessel but they will not give her up. The Privateer & Prize went around the E end this afternoon for N. York. The Privateer took several Wood men but released them all.

April 7, 1782

...The Privateer that was at the Barr last Thursday & Friday was up the Cod of the Bay middle afternoon. headed for the Point towards night.

April 12, 1782

...Hathaway & Meader sailed 7 weeks ago today for Philadelphia with a load of Oyl were taken & carried into N. York they have both got home.

April 28, 1782

...Before sunset yesterday Levi Barlow with 10 men in a boat from the other side came here. Capt. Nash had hired a Vessel of my father to carry him to some British port (Silv Coffin was bound master) they were near ready to sail this Barlow having a Commission & supposing her to be Capt Nash's property seized her & carried her off 11 clock last night the Selectmen & a number of the principal men used all their endeavours to prevent his carrying her away but all to no effect.

May 5, 1782

...An American Privateer came into the harbour at noon one Carver Commands her she belongs at Bedford — the Privateer went out of the harbour before noon May 6 — met with no encouragement. 'Tis said she came after south sea [Nantucket Sound?] men and their property.

June 8, 1782

...Levi Barlow went up the Harbour in his Mill this afternoon (he has been in the Harbour & about the Island for 8 or 10 days) they were anchored by William Hussey's house when we got up.

June 9, 1782

...News is that there is a large Fleet of Britains & Refugees at the Vineyard taking off sheep & cattle promising to pay for them.

June 13, 1782

...There is a schooner at the Bar (came there since noon) which is said to be a york Privateer I imagine frd [friend?] Barlow shakes in his shoes.

June 14, 1782

...Middle of the afternoon the Privateer came over the Barr & came into the harbour anchored near the L wharf -Barlow on seeing them enter the harbour onriged his Mill stove a Hole in her & retreated with his people to the head of the L wharf where he made a breast Work with Wood in order (as he pretended) to defend himself but the inhabitants instantly destroyed it on which he & his people wisely took to their heels out of Town not letting the grass grow under their Feet—the people out of the N. York Privateer landed on the S wharf & immediately destroyed Barlow's mill & then persued him & his People out of Town with all speed. They got sight of Barlow & several of his people but their having so much the start they dogged into the swamps where they hid & were not any of them to be found. The Refugees behav'd very civil not hurting anyone—'tis said that some of Barlow's men hid under houses some in swamps & some got on to Tuckanuck [Tuckernut Island].

June 15, 1782

...The york Privateer went out of the harbour some time in the night past & is no where in sight today. Hannah Gage came last night with Sears—were taken, by the Privateer treated very handsomely & let go. They took several little vessels but sot them all at Liberty. Major Bourn's son of Sandwich was first Lieut on Board—he was on shoar & in our shop yesterday—Barlow & his people crawl'd out of their Holes one after another today & before night got on board a little Vessel & sot out for the Main. The Refugees found Barlow's swivels & sails yesterday & carried them off.

June 18, 1782

...The york Privateer that was in the harbour last week was off the south side yesterday chased Silas Paddack on shoar south side (he was from the West Indies) went on board the Vessel & fired her. People went down & attempted to get on board to put out the fire—but the Privateer fired on them & kept them off for some time, but after a while the Privateer left her, the People went on board & put out the fire & got the most of the cargo on shoar. A few hogsheads of molasses was burnt. The Vessel's stern was most wholly burnt—her main deck was mostly burnt. The Privateer chas'd several Vessels off that were bound here.

June 22, 1782

...Lot Dimick in an American Privateer came in here this morn—soon after noon a small British schooner Privateer came to the Barr. Dimick took a small sloop went off showing only 2 men on Deck (20 went off). They ran alongside the schooner. The schooner fired on them slightly wounding Levi Barlow (he came here with Dimick). Dimick & his people immediately rose, fired on the schooner, ran alongside & rush'd on board, took her without further resistance. Both vessels came into the harbour—the Capt of the schooner is thought to be mortally wounded. & one more slightly wounded. Dimick went away before night with his Prize & Prisoners, all but the Capt.

August 15, 1782

...Levi Barlow with several armed men came to this Island 2 or 3 days ago (in pursuit of Prey). This afternoon Barlow with his crew went from here not meeting with any success—on his way westward not far from this Island they met with a boat which they pretend they thought to be a Refugee—they chased her she supposing them to be Refugees endeavour'd to make her escape but finding that impossible hove too—they ran alongside fired several guns—they own they discovered them to be Americans immediately after the boats were alongside & Barlow in his supposed enemy's boat demanding of the Capt. his Papers. One Swift one of Barlow's Pirats Put up his gun & fired at the Capt. wounded him in the Belly—Swift owns that he knew them to be Americans before he fired & the only excuse he pretends to make for himself is that he heard somebody say fire—both boats immediately put into the harbour, got in about 9 o'clock. Sent immediately for the Doctors—but they thought his wounds mortal—the Bullet went into his Belly & came out at his back...His name is Wood, a Bedford man.... He was taken about 2 years ago & carried into Philadelphia & there married about 5 months ago, He procured him a boat & a load of flour & went to Bedford to see his widow mother & his relations hearing that Flour sold well here was bound here to sell his provision when these pirates met him. [Cap't Wood died the next day.]

August 18, 1782

...Barlow came in last night & took McFarland's Vessel that was in the harbour. McFarland came in here in a Flag. She sail'd last may from Bermuda a Flag for here with Prisoners for the East & for the West. The Eastern Prisoners rose just before they got in & carried the Vessel down to Portsmouth from there she was sent to Boston & has there been detained till the week before last—when she was sot at liberty & was a Flag to some British Port. He put in here in distress, his Vessel not being fit to go to sea. Got leave of the Selectmen to heave down & fit his Vessel—last night he bound out when Barlow with his Banditti stopt him & has carried him this morning to Falmouth—his pretence for taking him is that she being a flag had no right to go into a harbour & heave down.

September 1, 1782

...An American shaving mill came into the harbour this afternoon.

September 2, 1782

...After 12 clock Absalum came up here on horseback for to desire Mr. Fanning to go immediately to Town, Levi Barlow being at my Father's seizing the goods &c. Mr. Fanning sot out on horseback, I followed him in the Calash—Levi Barlow with 2 others went into my Father's shop & then (pretended) in the name of the Commonwealth of this state to seize all the goods in the shop as British property—people began to gather & in a short time our street was lined with men women & children—Barlow began immediately to pull down the goods off the shelves & throw them down on the counter takeing an inventory of them—Persavel who is Barlow's Capt soon came in after him and a number of others.

Barlow went away to dinner & when he return'd was not suffer'd to come into the house again, the doors being fastened. 3 of the theifes in the house & a number of the inhabitants indoors & out—when Mr. Fanning came down he endeavoured to make peace, offer'd to Persival to give Bonds for the goods which offer was accepted—when I got into Town People had generally dispersed out of the streets. Persival & one of his Crew were in the shop, Roland Gelston takeing an inventory of the goods at mother's request. A number of People in the house & shop just before they had finished taking the inventory.

Mr. Fanning demanded of Persival his commission which he with reluctance shewed him. Mr. Fanning on reading it found he had no power to take any thing above high water mark—P. F. told him that as a frd [friend] he advised Persival to stop & proceed no further. He seemed all at once to recollect himself, told P. F. he would not take any bonds & on leaving the shop, desired the people present to bear witness that he did not seize the goods—while they were in the shop, they were insulted as much as it was possible for people to be—they went into Mr. Beanes & Timo Folgers shop & there in the name of the Commonwealth seized there goods. Timo Folger poled them out of doors & fastened his doors upon them, they were served the same at Beanes—many of the inhabitants shewed by their countenances the joy they had on the occasion—things was pretty peaceable after they left the shop—Mr. Butler armed his house.

September 3, 1782

...Percival and his Crew went off today, carried a small lumber vessel with them that came into the harbor a few nights ago.

September 16, 1782

...Persival came on the Island today.

October 2, 1782

...A york Privateer Brigg anchored at the Barr this morn. Young Husbands Commanded her; he has been here before.

October 5, 1782

...The Privateer that has been at the Barr for some days past went from there today. She has taken several little vessels, some have ransom'd for a small matter, others she has taken some trifal from & let go, she has not carried off one -tis said she fir'd a Vessel after she sailed at a great distance but just discernable.

October 12, 1782

...Gideon Gardner was coming Through miscecit [Muskeget] yesterday in a Brigg (loaded with sugar, molasses &c) & was chased ashoar by a Privateer—he does not know whether an American or British as she quited her chase after he struck the shoar—he came to the Island in his boat last night—a number of boats went away this morn to take out his load.

December 2, 1782

An armed schooner & 2 unarmed sloops & one armed from N. York anchor'd at the Barr this forenoon—common Fame says they are loaded with goods—several of the people are on shoar.

December 3, 1782

...The 4 British Vessels came into the harbour last night—the famous Goldsberry is on board—one Eben Coffin (originally from Boston) came in one of the Vessels.

December 10, 1782

...The York Vessels sail'd this afternoon—have carried away some oyl. (s.242)

Such is the story of the raids of the Refugees, the British and the Americans during the year 1782, as portrayed by a young woman of 23, impressible and clearly not enthusiastically attached to the American cause, her feelings being strongly influenced by her immediate environment, but from her standpoint giving an excellent idea of the constant strain the people of Nantucket were under, not knowing the day or the hour when some new raid would be attempted, liable to the depredations of all three and powerless not only physically but by the teachings of their religion, to ward off the predatory incursions of either....

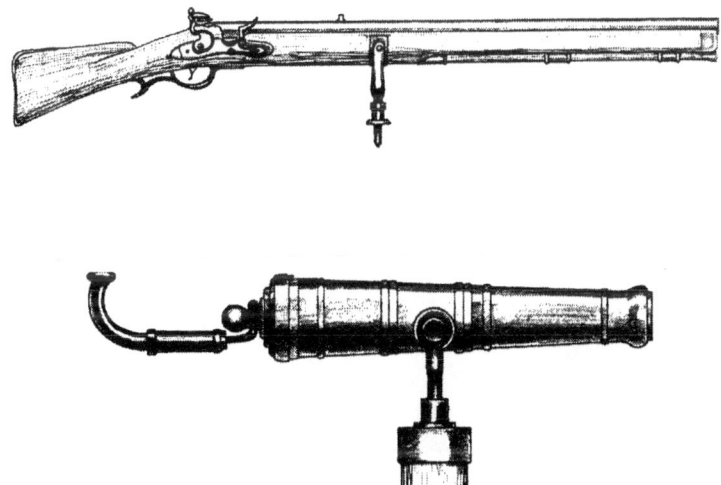

Flintlock Wall Gun (above); Swivel Gun (below).

A Sail in the Distance.

14

Epilogue

**From an Address of Dr. Andrew P. Peabody
To the Bostonian Society — April, 1888**

There was at the same time in and about Boston a large mob element professing ardent patriotism, and commonly regarded as auxiliary to the movements which issued in the war of independence. I believe that this element was in every respect as harmful and detrimental as it was unlawful and immoral; that it thinned the ranks of the patriots, disgusted many worthy citizens with the cause which it professed to further, and was of unspeakable benefit to the neighboring provinces of Nova Scotia and New Brunswick in giving them from among the exiles from Massachusetts the best judges, lawyers, clergymen, and men of elegant culture that they have ever had, including not a few graduates of Harvard College. (b.174)

From Lecky's *England in the Eighteenth Century*

The American Revolution, like most others, was the work of an energetic minority who succeeded in committing an undecided and fluctuating majority to courses for which they had little love, and leading them step by step to a position from which it was impossible to recede. (b.184)

Extract from Freeman,
History of Cape Cod, Annals of Falmouth (1862)

In 1781, May 18; the town petitioned the General Court "for relief from the enemy infesting the coast." To guard the shores, 24 men were employed night and day; but no adequate protection was afforded. It has ever been the misfortune of the Cape, that, in times of danger from invasion, it has received no aid from government, whilst, notwithstanding its peculiarly exposed situation, it has been expected besides its contribution to the naval service, to sustain its full share of the public burden, and also to furnish its full quota of recruits for the land-service abroad.

There are always, in times of war or insurrection, some who side with the enemy, and luxuriate in their country's calamity. In localities where they may easily find refuge, or protection, domestic foes are emboldened, and will be sure to find numerous sympathizers among those who,--

> In moderation placing all their glory,
> While Tories call them Whigs, and Whigs say Tory,-

are, after all, the severest trial against which true patriotism is called to contend.... (f.II-462)

April 16, 1782, Falmouth

...A company of 26 men was employed nightly to guard the coast; for which service they were paid 3s. per night. The records from this period, are barren of interest for several years.... (f.II-462)

References and Codes

Code	Reference
(a)	André, John. *Journal – Operations of the British Army under Lieutenant Generals Sir William Howe and Sir Henry Clinton June 1777 to November 1778*. Tarrytown, NY: William Abbatt, 1930.
(b)	Bliss, William Root. *Colonial Times on Buzzard's Bay*. Boston: Houghton, Mifflin and Co.; Cambridge: The Riverside Press, 1889. Reprint, Westminster, MD: Heritage Books, Inc., 2002.
(c)	Coggins, Jack. *Ships and Seamen of the American Revolution*. Harrisburg, PA: Stackpole Books, 1969. Reprint, New York: Dover, 2002.
(e)	Emerson, Amelia Forbes. *Early History of Naushon Island*, Boston: Howland & Co., 2nd edition, 1981.
(fI)	Freeman, Frederick. *History of Cape Cod, v. I – The Annals of Barnstable County*. Boston: Rand & Avery, 1858.
(fII)	Freeman, Frederick. *History of Cape Cod, v. II – The Annals of the Thirteen Towns of Barnstable County*. Boston: Rand & Avery, 1862.
(h)	Historic Print and Map Company. *New England Revolutionary War Era Maps*. www.historicarchive.com.
(i)	http://www.linzeefamilyassn.org/bios.htm#captainlinzee
(j)	Ray Sterner, Applied Physics Laboratory, Johns Hopkins University, licensed by North Star Science and Technology LLC.
(k)	Allen, Gardner W. *A Naval History of the American Revolution*. Williamstown, MA: Corner House, (1913) 1970.
(l)	Lincoln, Joseph C. and Harold Bertt. *Cape Cod Yesterdays*, Little, Brown and Company, 1937.

(m) Munson, William T. "Privateering in Vineyard Sound in the Revolutionary War," Woods Hole Historical Collection, *Spritsail*, v. 4, no. 1, Winter 1999.

(n) *Naval Documents of the American Revolution*. Washington DC: U.S. Government Printing Office.

Volume	Editor	Pub. date	ID number
1	Clark, W. B.	1964	LC 64-60087
2	Clark, W. B	1966	LC 64-60087
3	Clark, W. B.	1968	LC 64-60087
4	Clark, W. B.	1969	LC 64-60087
5	Morgan, W. J.	1970	LC 64-60087
6	Morgan, W. J.	1972	LC 64-60087
7	Morgan, W. J.	1976	LC 64-60087
8	Morgan, W. J.	1980	LC 64-60087
9	Morgan, W. J.	1986	LC 64-60087
10	Crawford, M. J.	1996	LC 64-60087
11	Crawford, M. J.	2005	LC 64-60087

(o) The On-Line Institute for Advanced Loyalist Studies. http://www.royalprovincial.com/index.htm

(p) Personal collection of the compiler.

(r) Rago, Joe, "Alarm at Falmouth 1779," Unpublished monograph in the collection of the Falmouth Historical Society, circa 1992.

(s) Starbuck, Alexander. *The History of Nantucket*. Boston: Goodspeed, 1924.

(w) Meadowcroft, Enid L. *When Nantucket Men Went Whaling*. Champaign, IL: Garrard, 1996.

(y) Emmet Collection, Miriam and Ira D. Wallach Division of Art, Prints and Photographs, The New York Public Library, Astor, Lenox and Tilden Foundations.

Lovell, R. A. *Sandwich: A Cape Cod Town*. Taunton: Sullwold, 1996.

Railton, Authur R. *The History of Martha's Vineyard*. Beverly, MA: Commonwealth Editions, 2006.

INDEX

----, Absalum, 143
Abercrombie, Gen., 121
Acushnet River, 93–95, 97
Adams
  Abigail, 61
  John, 61
Aliquumvisit Harbor, 80
Allen, Maria, 62–63
Ambuscade, 64–65
Anderson, Lt., 64
André, John, 85–86
Aponeganset Neck, 88
Apthorp, William, 103
Arbuthnot, Adm., 137
Ayscough, James, 39–40, 44, 46
Bacon, 3
Bahama Islands, 127
Baillie, Capt., 88
Banker, Mr., 130
Barker
  John, 9
  Josiah, 49
Barker's Harbour [Parker's Harbor? i.e., Little Harbor?], 89
Barlow, Jesse, 19–20
  Levi, 139–143
Barnard, William, 138
Barnstable, Mass., xi, 1–2, 5–6, 20, 25–27, 40, 43–44, 102, 105, 134
Barton, William, 46
Bassett
  Barachiah, 29, 45, 58–61, 121
  Bart, 42
  Fortunatus, 45
Batles, Daniel, 42
Beane
  John, 139
  Mr., 143
Bedford, Mass., 17, 75, 78, 86–87, 93, 95–99, 102, 121, 139, 142
Bermuda, 142
Bliss, William Root, 5
Block Island, 68, 86
Blossom, James, 45
Blowers, 131
Boston Harbor, 14
Boston, Mass., 5, 9, 12–13, 15, 17, 28, 35, 40, 42, 46, 48–49, 53, 55, 57–58, 69–70, 75, 98–99, 102, 112, 122, 130, 139, 142, 144
Boston Neck, 12
Bourn, Maj., 141
Bowdoin, James, 21
Bowin, 82
Briggs, Nathaniel, 6
Bristol, Mass., 102
Brown, John, 46
Browne, Capt., 88
Bumpus, Salathiel, 6

Bunker Hill, 102
Burgess, 35
Burgoyne, 75
Butler, Mr., 143
Buzzards Bay, 19, 30, 41, 69, 78, 80–81, 86, 88, 93–94
Byron, 98
Cambridge Marsh, 9–10
Cambridge, Mass., 18, 31, 57
Capan, 130
Cape Breton, 127
Cape Cod, Mass., ix, 18, 41, 130
Cape-Ann [Cape Ann], 66
Carisfort, 86–87, 89
Carver, 139
Castle William [Castle Island], 48
Champion, 15
Charlestown, Mass., 10, 12
Charlotte, 133
Chase, Deborah, 113
Chatham, Mass., xi
Chilmarck, 92
Christie, James, 54, 57
Clarisfort, 93, 96–97
Clark's Cove, 86, 93
Clark's Neck, 87
Cleveland, Stephen, 57
Clinton, Gen. Sir Henry, 75, 85, 93, 96, 126
Coatue Point, 48
Coffin
  Ebenezer, 144
  Kezia, 36
  Richard, 35
  Silv, 139
  Thomas A., 131

Collier, Sir George, 126–127
Concord, Mass., 9–10, 12–13, 102
Cooke, Nicholas, 46
Coore, Capt., 78
Cornwallis, 88
Crane's Mills, 87, 95
Crocker, Tim, 42
Crosby, 138
Cuttyhunk Island, 74, 78
Daggett
  Mr., 62
  Polly, 62–63
Danbury, Connecticut, 102
Dark, James, 73
Dartmouth, Mass., 18–21, 31, 60–61
Davis
  Daniel, 133
  Joshua, 24–25, 30, 35
  Melatiah, 45
  Noah, 42
Dawson, Capt., 115–116
Defence, 62, 121
Dependence, 88
DePeyster, Capt., 99, 114
D'Estaing, 98
Diamond, 64–65
Digby, Adm., 137
Dimick [Dimmick], Joseph, 133
  Lot, 141
Dimmick
  Col., 134
  Joseph, 45–46, 119–122, 135, 137–138
  Lot, 119, 121

Index 153

Dimock [Dimmick], Maj., 105, 107–108
Dimuck [Dimmick], Joseph, 70
Doctor, 25–27, 29
Dogget, Maj., 54
Dominica, 24
Donkin, Col., 87, 92
Dorchester, Mass., 48
Dornett, Mr., 129
Dow, Capt., 114, 128
Durfee, Thomas, 60–61
Dyer, Hannah, 100
Eason, Peleg, 138
Eatons Neck, 129–130
Edgartown, 53, 55, 134
Egery, Daniel, 19
Egry, Daniel, 21
Eldridge, Barnabas, 134
Elizabeth Islands, ix–xi, 14–15, 17, 20, 27–29, 31, 41, 45–46, 59–60, 64–65, 68–69, 71, 77–78, 81, 130–131
Experiment, 114
Fair Haven, 87–88, 93, 97
Falcon, 14–15, 17–20, 22, 24–25
Falmouth, Mass., ix–xi, 14, 29, 36, 38, 41–42, 45–46, 65, 70–71, 74, 77, 80–83, 89, 95, 99–100, 103, 105, 107–108, 112, 114, 121, 132–135, 137–138, 142, 148
Fanning
  Col., 131
  Edmund, 99, 102
  Mr., 143
  Mrs., 138
  Phineas, 38
  Rand, 38

Fanshaw, 97
  Robert, 86, 89–91, 96
Fearing
  Brig. Gen., 97
  Noah, 6
Fielding, Charles, 64–65, 68
Fish
  Capt., 105
  Lt., 77
  Samuel, 42
Fitch, Timothy, 112
Florida, 127
Folger
  Abishai, 49
  Frederick, 49
  Timothy, 49, 132, 143
Ford, Capt., 78
Forsyth, Capt., 114
Fowey, 88
Francis, 53
Freeman
  Col., 45, 105, 107–108, 112
  Nantucket, Mass., 81
  Nathaniel, 2–5, 13, 19–20, 28, 35, 43, 50–51, 83
  Samuel, 70
Furnell, William, 53
Gage, 12
  Gen., 24, 35, 102
  Gov., 5
  Hannah, 140
Galatea, 130
Gambier, Rear Adm., 96, 98
Gardiners Island, 128
Gardner, Gideon, 144
Garth, 133
Gefferina, G., 15

Gelston
  Elizabeth, 47
  Roland, 51, 143
  Samuel, 40, 43, 45–47, 49–51, 112, 132
  Sandwich, Mass., 48
General Leslie, 99, 114–115, 135
General Mathew, 114
General Prescott, 115
George, 115
Georgia, 58
Germain, Lord George, 75, 96, 98
Geyer, 35
Gibbs, John, 6
Gilston [Gelston], Samuel, 60
Goldsberry, 144
Goldsborough, Mr., 129
Grannis, John, 45, 60
Gravelly Island, 48–49
Graves
  Adm., 102
  Sam, 15
  Samuel, 14
Green, 133
Gregg, Lt., 64
Grey, Gen., 87–90, 93, 96–97, 131
Grieder, James Everett, 47
Guadaloupe, 66
Haerlem, 72–73, 75, 78–80
Hallett, Samuel, 45
Hamilton, Alexander, 86
Hancock, Gov., 122
Harriot, 55, 114
Harvard College, 148

Hatch
  Silas, 71
  Silas Jr., 121
Hathaway, 139
Heath, William, 57
Henry, Capt., 86
Hingham, Mass., 40
Holland, Richard, 99
Holmes, Abraham, 1, 6
Holmes Hole [Vineyard Haven], 15, 22, 24, 29, 39, 47, 57, 62, 72, 75, 89–90, 92–93, 95, 102, 108, 134
Howe
  Gen. Sir William, 75, 86
  Vice Adm. Richard, Lord, 68, 84, 92–93, 98
Hull, Mass., 70
Hunter, 130
Huntington Harbour, 127–128
Hussey
  Christopher Jr., 120
  Stephen, 38
  William, 140
Hutchinson, Gov., 100, 102
Hyannis, Mass., 74, 81, 133–135
Jeffers, Mr., 129
Jenkins
  Jonathan, 35–36, 41
  Thomas, 112
Jennigan, William, 135
Jones, Elisha, 129
  Robinson, 121
  Thomas, 69, 134
Kingfisher, 17, 31
Kingston, Mass., 13, 30

Knight, John, 72
Knox, William, 98
Lawrence, Fred, xi
Leonard, George, xi, 99, 102, 104, 108, 112, 114–115, 120, 128–130, 132, 134–135
Leslie, 133
Lexington, Mass., 9–10, 12, 102
Lindley [Linzee], John, 21
Linsey [Linzee], John, 19, 27–28
Linzee, John, 14–15, 17, 22, 24–26
Linzey [Linzee], John, 20
Lloyds Neck, 130
Long Island Sound, 86
Loring, Commodore, 58
Lorrance, John, 132
Lothrop, Lt., 44
Lovell
   Christopher, 40
   David, 40
   Mr., 43
   Shubael, 39–40, 43
Lowther, William, 53
Macartney, John, 64–65, 68
MacFarland, 142
MacPherson, Capt., 114
Macy, Reuben, 138
   Zacceus, 49
Malsburg, Friederich von der, 78
Mannantha [Menemsha], 15
Manter
   Jeremiah, 45
   Parnel, 62–63
Manter's Hill, 62–63
Marblehead, Mass., 10, 121

Marr, John, 127
Marsh, Edward, 58
Martha's Vineyard, Mass., ix–xi, 15, 17–18, 31, 39, 45, 47, 53, 57–58, 62, 75, 79, 85, 88, 94, 96, 99, 102–103, 108, 112, 128–130, 132, 135, 140
Martha's Vineyard Sound, 64, 72–73, 81, 89, 94–95, 114, 132
Mary, 73
Massachusetts, 147
Matthews, Isaac, 134
Mayhew, Hilyard, 60
McClean, Capt., 114
McPherson's Wharf, 87, 95
Meader, 139
Meiggs, Ebenezer, 28
Menotomy [Arlington], Mass., 10
Middleboro, Mass., 2
Mitchell, Richard, 38
Montagu, James, 31
Murarius, Lt., 79–80
Murray, 112
   Daniel, 99
   Sir James, 86
Muskeget, 48, 144
Muskeket [Muskeget], 49
Nantucket, Mass., ix–x, 19, 22, 24, 30, 35–36, 38–41, 43, 45–46, 48–51, 72, 74, 89, 92, 102, 108, 111–115, 120, 125, 127–128, 130, 132–133, 137–138, 145
Nantucket Shoals, 54–55
Nantucket Sound, 73
Narishawn [Naushon], 126
Narragansett Bay, 77, 104

Narriganset [Narragansett], 125
Nash, Capt., 139
Nashavinna [Nashawena] Island, 80
Nashawene (Slocum's Island), x, 78
Naushon Island, x, 20–21, 29, 41–42, 46, 63–65, 68, 70, 78, 80–81, 130,
New Brunswick, 147
New London, Connecticut, 75, 86, 93
New York, 55, 68, 90, 116, 126–127, 135, 138–140, 144
Newport, Rhode Island, 17, 21, 36, 46–47, 54, 63, 75, 81–82, 98–99, 102, 104, 112, 114–115, 126, 128–129, 131, 135
Nickerson, Commissary, 72
Noddle's Island, 48
Noman's Land, 125, 130
Nonamesset Island, 78, 82, 107–108, 112
North, Lord, 13
Norton
  Beriah, 53–54
  Col., 135
  Henry Franklin, 62
Nova Scotia, 147
Nye
  Benj., 66
  Capt., 82
  Elisha, 20, 25–26, 28, 45, 69, 71–72
  John, 82
  Joseph, 43, 77

Nye (cont.)
  Stephen Jr., 45
Old Town [Edgartown] Harbor, 95, 129–130, 134–135
Oliver Cromwell, 127
Oliver, Peter, 102
Orrock, Weymse, 55–57
Otis
  Col., 3, 43
  James, 53
  Joseph, 133–135
  Maj., 5
Oxford, Mass., 97
Oyster Island, 134
Paddack, Silas, 141
  Stephen, 132
Paddock, Master, 15
Palmer, 133
  Jo, 42
  Polly, 61
Parker
  Capt., 55
  Peter, 64, 68
Peabody, Andrew P., 147
Peas, John, 135
Peggy, 60
Penikese Island, 72, 78
Percival/Persival, Capt., 143–144
Percy, Earl, 13
Perry, Samuel, 133
  Townsman, 82
Peshtemet Island, 78
Pesktenset Island, 80
Pesque [Pasque] Island, 105
Phenex [*Phoenix*], 53

Philadelphia, Pennsylvania, 41, 61, 77, 139, 142
Phoenix, 55
Pigot, Sir Robert, 88
Pitcairn, Maj., 9, 12
Plymouth, Mass., 13, 30, 46, 50, 57, 61, 100, 102, 112
Point Judith, 125
Portsmouth, 142
Prescott, Gen., 115–116, 129
Preston, 15, 133
Providence, 73–74
Providence, Rhode Island, 46, 69, 121
Provincetown, Mass., xi
Prudence [Prudence Island], 125
Prudence Island, 104
Quicks Hole, 72, 82, 88, 94
Quidnecit, 126
Raisonable, 127
Read
  John, 64
  Mr., 82
Reskatemeth Island, 27
Restoration, 103, 127, 133
Rhode Island, 41, 44, 55, 64, 78, 82, 86, 88, 92, 102, 104, 108, 112, 114, 135
Rhode Island Harbor, 64
Riddle, 138
Ried, Mr., 79
Rising Empire, 61
Robinson
  Elisha, 28
  Jeremiah, 28, 65
  William, 28

Robinson's Hole, 21, 65
Robisson, 79–80
Rochester, Mass., 1–2, 5
Rodman, Samuel, 139
Rose, 21
Rotch [Roach], William, 35, 115–116, 132, 138
  William Jr, 139
Roxbury, Mass., 57
Roye, Mr., 129
Ruggles, Brig., 112
Russel, Ben, 138
Russell, John, 45
Rutland, 112
Salem, Mass., 10, 12, 57
Sally, 75, 114
Sandwich [Bourne], Mass., 2, 5–6, 13, 19–20, 28, 43, 45, 77, 81–82, 105, 108, 133, 141
Savage, Capt., 129
Scarborough, 58
Sconticut Neck, 97
Scorpion, 88, 95
Seaflower, 121
Sears, 140
Shaw, James, 45, 54–55
Shelter Island, 38
Sherborn [Sherburne] (Nantucket), x, 45
Sherbourne [Nantucket Village], 126
Shimmo, 48
Shiverick, Nathll, 42
Sicchio, Mary, xiii
Sinclair, Patrick, 64
Skonticut Neck, 87
Slocomb, John, 105

Smith
  Benj., 45, 54–55
  Col., 12
  Lt. Coll., 9
  Nathan, 45
Sopers, Capt., 30
South Kingston, 126
Southampton, Long Island, 47
Spectacle Island, 48
Spelling, Capt., 114
Sphynx, 78–79, 81
Spooner, Walter, 61
St. Vincents, 25
Starbuck, 132
  Daniel, 120
  Samuel, 36, 115–116
Stiles, Ezra, 21
Stirling, Lt. Col., 92
Stonington, Mass., 133
Story, William, 50–51
Sullivan, Gen., 81, 98, 104
Swan, 17, 39, 45, 78
Swift, 142
  Capt., 105
  Ephraim, 104
  Manassah, 104
  Manasses, 135
  Mrs. Manassah, 105
Talor, Joseph, 114
Tappan, 85
Tarpaulin Cove, 14–15, 20, 24–27, 31, 41–42, 46, 59–60, 65–66, 70, 73, 81, 89, 104, 119–120
Taunton, Mass., 18
Taylor, Joseph, 128–129
Temple, Robert, 48
Thacher, Dr., 85
Thaxter, Mr., 130
Ticonderoga, 121
Times, 114
Trevett, John, 73
Truro, Mass., 59
Tucker
  John, 27
  Joseph, 28
Tuckernuck [Tuckernut Island], 48
Tuckernut Island, 140
Tuckers [Pasque] Island, 28
Tupper, 82
  Benj., 116
  Benjamin, 115, 128–129, 132
  Eldad, 111
Turk's Island, 138
Unicorn, 62–63
Union, 78–79, 121
Upham, Joshua, 129, 131
Valenti [*Violenti*], 58
Vaughan, Gen., 102
Vinyard Haven Harbor, 72
Violenti, 57
Wallace, James, 21
Wanton, Joseph, 64
Wareham, Mass., xi, 2, 5–6, 81, 97
Washington, 125
Washington, George, 43–44, 57, 75, 85, 98
Watertown, Mass., 30, 44, 53, 57, 60
Watson, W., 13
Wellen, Richard, 54
Wentworth, Gov., 102
West Indies, 18–19, 98, 113, 141

West, William, 46–47
White, Ebenezer, 50–51
Williams, Lemuel, 61
Wing
 James, 135
 John, 28
 Simeon, 19–20
 Thomas, 19
Winslow, 3
 Col., 114
 Edward, 99–100, 104
 Edward (Ned), 100, 102–103, 108, 112, 126
 Hannah (Dyer), 100
 Ned, 13
 Pelham, 112
Winyaw, North Carolina, 57
Wood, Capt., 142
Woods Hole, 42, 83, 89, 104, 107, 119–120, 134
Worcester, Mass., 18
Yarmouth, Mass., 135

About the Author

FREDERICK V. LAWRENCE, JR.

Frederick V. Lawrence, Jr. was born in Woods Hole, Massachusetts, in 1938. He attended primary and secondary school first in Woods Hole and later in Falmouth, Massachusetts. After spending his Junior and Senior high school years at Moses Brown in Providence, Rhode Island, Fred entered Haverford College in 1956 and received a B. S. in Civil Engineering in 1960 from Swarthmore College. He attended graduate school at the Massachusetts Institute of Technology where he specialized in Civil Engineering receiving an S. M. degree in 1962 and a Civil Engineer's Degree (C. E.) in 1965. In 1968, he obtained a doctorate (Sc. D.) from MIT in the area of Materials Science.

Fred joined the faculties of Metallurgy and Mining Engineering and Civil Engineering at the University of Illinois at Urbana in 1968. Fred taught courses in welding and materials engineering and researched the mechanical properties of welds and the influence of weld discontinuities on the their tensile and fatigue properties. From 1976 to 1989, Fred was the Director of the UIUC Materials Engineering Research Laboratory. He was the Co-editor of the ASCE Journal of Materials in Civil Engineering from 1988 to 1996. From 1996 to 2004, Fred was the Associate Head of the Department of Civil Engineering and Environmental Engineering. Fred retired from the university on May 15, 2004 and is now a Professor Emeritus.

In retirement, Fred spends summers in his family home in Waquoit, Massachusetts, sailing and researching Cape Cod history, and spends his winters in Urbana, Illinois, playing early music and directing the University of Illinois German Choir.

www.ingramcontent.com/pod-product-compliance
Lightning Source LLC
Chambersburg PA
CBHW050816160426
43192CB00010B/1782